NAVAJO WEAVING WAY

NAVAJO WEAVING WAY
The Path from Fleece to Rug

Noël Bennett ❧ Tiana Bighorse

Photographs by John Running

INTERWEAVE PRESS

Cover photograph, Grace Homer, weaving; by John Running
Text © 1997, Shared Horizons, Inc.
Photographs © 1997, John Running
Book design, Elizabeth R. Mrofka

Interweave Press, Inc.
201 East Fourth Street
Loveland, Colorado 80537-5655
USA

Printed in the United States of America

Library of Congress Cataloging-in-Publication Data
Bennett, Noël, 1939–
    Navajo weaving way : the path from fleece to rug / Noël Bennett and Tiana Bighorse.
      p. cm.
    Includes bibliographical references and index.
    ISBN 1-883010-30-6
    1. Navajo textile fabrics.   2. Hand weaving—Southwest, New– Patterns.
    3. Textile design—Southwest, New.   I. Bighorse, Tiana, 1917–   II. Title.
E99.N3B488   1997
746' .089'972—dc21   97-11687
                                                CIP

First Printing: IWP—7.5M:597:QUE

Dedication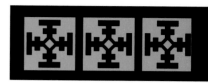

To Tiana's mother, Bertha Whitehair Bighorse,
and to Tiana's grandmother
and great-grandmother
and great-great-grandmother,
for keeping alive past traditions for future Navajo
weavers

and
in commemoration of Tiana's eightieth birthday,
June 10, 1997

 # Acknowledgments

Navajo Weaving Way represents the coming together of many diverse energies. Specifically I wish to honor:

Jim Wakeman, walking / working / writing / dreaming partner.
And friend.

Audrey Moore, exquisite weaver / tireless teacher / manuscript consultant.
And friend.

Timothy M. Sheehan, steadfast legal consultant.
And friend.

Linda Ligon and Interweave Press
Riki Darling and Kim Mumbower

Valued colleagues:
John Gerber
Ann Hedlund
Susan McGreevy
Marian Rodee
Gloria Ross
Leora Smith
Joe Ben Wheat
Mark Winter

And mentors:
Jackson Clark
Harry King
Michael McGuire
Patricia Clark Smith

The Navajo women who have shared their weaving craft:

Betty Begay • Mary Ann Begay
Stella Begay • Mrs. Jimmy Boone
Diane Calamity • Rose Laughter
Mary Leonard • 'Asdzán Łitsoi
Wanda MacDonald • Edna Maloney
Jean Mann • Sarah Natani
Narcissa Rose Patrick • Bertha Pinto
Running Woman • Bessy Sellers
Lydia Smallcanyon • Mary Alice Smiley
Bertha Stevens • Pearl Sunrise
Rachael Tahawney • Nedra Todichiinii
Nina Toledo • Mrs. Tom C. Tolino
Ella Tsinnie • Helen Nesbah Tsinnie
Angie Tunney • Carolyn Tunney

Tiana's children:

Billy Butler
Raymond Butler, Sr.
Sallie Butler-Maloney
Maybelle Butler Weeks
Leonard Glenn Butler
Harvey A. Butler
Loretta Butler

And Clara, who introduced us.

Tiana's brothers:

Dan Bighorse
Glenn Bighorse
Floyd Bighorse

Table of Contents

Tiana Bighorse

 # Introductions

"Beauty is truth, truth beauty,"—that is all

Ye know on earth, and all ye need to know.

—John Keats

Thirty years ago, with an M.A. in Fine Arts and a three-year-old son, I am at Little Bear's Trading Post outside Gamerco, Arizona. My husband had just signed on to do alternative military service with the Indian Health Hospital in Tuba City. Past the sacks of fry-bread flour and the glass cases of pawned turquoise, I see my first Navajo rug. The texture is nubby, the plant dyes earthy and glowing. And in the abstract geometrics I see the vision of an ordered cosmos.

A year later, I am part of the Bighorse-Butler family. Under Tiana's caring mentoring, I am learning to shear sheep, card, spin, and dye. My loom is my easel; the warp, my canvas.

Three years later, Tiana and I collaborate on our first book, *Working With the Wool: How to Weave a Navajo Rug*. We write it to keep young Navajo women close to their culture. To help non-Navajos appreciate the beauty of the Navajo weaving process. It is a legacy—Tiana's mother's stories.

The next year I am invited to teach Navajo weaving at the National Handweavers' Conference. Going from the Navajo reservation to Convergence '72 thrusts me into culture shock. Suddenly I'm among thousands of weavers and hundreds of vendors selling everything from 14-harness Jacquard looms to back-straps. By now I know I love weaving; envision myself doing it the rest of my life. Here is my chance to find a "real" loom.

I talk to manufacturers, visit workshops, try out the looms on display. But they are clattery. Cumbersome. Expensive. They need elaborate paraphernalia: warping frames, shuttles, heddle threaders, bobbin winders, swifts, tensioners, spool racks. And more.

The more I look at the jumble of options, the more comforting is my Navajo loom back home. The process is direct; there is no mechanization between me and my art. The upright loom lets me see my design. It is inexpensive. Portable. Beautiful! Everything about it has heart.

In the ensuing years, Tiana and I collaborate many more times: *Designing with the Wool: Advanced Techniques in Navajo Weaving; Weaver's Pathway: A Clarification of the "Spirit Trail" in Navajo Weaving; Halo of the Sun: Stories Told and Retold.*

In 1975, while teaching workshops across the United States—and with little time to weave—I ask Glen Kaufman, Professor of Weaving at University of Georgia, to advise me as to which is the best tapestry loom for me.

"Why would you want to weave on any but the Navajo?"

"Because the sheds are slow. I want to be able to step on a pedal or pull a handle and have the shed work automatically." My friend looks thoughtful.

"You might reconsider. . . . One of the beauties of the Navajo loom is that it's a continuous warp. That means that when you're done weaving, your tapestry has a finished selvage on all four sides. And the fabric is reversible; the back is as good as the front. You can't do better."

Maybe I look doubtful, for he continues.

"When I weave one of my pieces, it may go faster. But when I get to the end, I still have a lot to do. I still have to thread in each cut end. Laboriously. Then back the fabric. Your weaving process may take longer. But when you're done, you're done. And you have a superior product. So clean. Logical. Self-contained."

Many years later, Tiana wants to make a book about her father's stories and asks me to help. Her father lived during The Long Walk when the U.S. Cavalry force-marched the Navajo People across New Mexico to Fort Sumner. It is a black period in American history, and few books report it accurately. For our 1990 collaboration, *Bighorse The Warrior,* Tiana is named "Navajo of the Year" and receives the Buddy Joe-Bojack Humanitarian Award.

Today, people ask if I'm still weaving. I smile and answer, "Yes!" Then add that whatever I'm doing—weaving yarns on a warp, words on a page, or colors on a canvas—Tiana and my spiritual loom speak to me, guide my life.

For Navajo weaving is meditative work that invites Woman into the energy center of the balanced universe. A place where everyday happenings merge with the mythical. Here sunlight shimmers through virginal tight-strung warp. Here Father Sky and Mother Earth unite. Here Spiderwoman weaves her tangled web. And Changing Woman / White Shell Woman— the primordium—prevails.

The Navajo Weaving Way is tangible and transcendent. It embraces silence and ritual. Family and heart. Shows us the spirituality of the ordinary. Offers balance and hope.

—*Noël Bennett*

I am a Navajo. My name is Tiana Bighorse. My hometown is Tuba City, Arizona. I belong to the Deer Springs clan born for the Rocky Gap clan, that is how we introduce ourselves in our way. I am eighty winters old. I went up to the ninth grade in the Tuba City Boarding School. Then my mother got sick. I have to take care of her for a whole year. I'm her only daughter and I got three brothers. There was nobody else to take care of her. Two very important things I learned from my mother: cooking corn flour in the Navajo way and how to weave a rug.

From the time I was little my mother was always weaving. My mother used to weave big rugs and she especially liked to make the Storm Pattern design. Five feet by seven feet was her regular rug size. When I was seven years old, I started to help her weave. I would sit by her and fill up the space where she left it for me. I could do this just in the plain areas. I thought I was doing it to see if I could, and my mother thought I was just playing around. But pretty soon I could really do it good and I began to get very interested in weaving. Finally she show me how to put the yarns in to make design and how to hook yarns together. I have a hard time with that hooking at the edge of the design.

I started school when I was eight years old. My mother put me to school then and after that

I have to go to school all the time. When I come home in the summertime, I help her with the weaving. One summer she told me to learn how to card wool and spin it. I have to do it by myself. She said, "I will not be by your side all your life—spinning wool and carding wool for you. You have to do it by yourself." I did learn it and I learned how to dye wool. I have to know by lifting the wool how much dye to put in. I sometimes make a mistake. That is how you learn something—if you know where you make a mistake.

My mother didn't put up a small loom for me to learn. She just tell me to sit by her and help her with what she is weaving. She likes to weave big rugs. She was a fast weaver and spinner. One day I decided to put up my own loom. Without her help I put up the warp and started my own loom. My mother was very proud of me. Finally I finish my own rug. It was a big one. I did it without nobody's help. I think to myself, "I have made it."

My mother died when I was twenty-two years old. This weaving had been coming through the family a long time before that. It was a century ago that the weaving was coming through my mother's family.

Nowadays there is lots of different kinds of design. But I still remember those old designs that my mother used to make. I like to weave these designs so they will not be forgotten. People used to make their own dresses and weave their own blankets. All the families know how to weave in those days because they need something to wear for themselves, and blankets for the family.

After that the government gave them clothes and blankets and food. From then on the weaving started to go away. Just a few families didn't forget to weave. My great-great-grandmother was one of them. She didn't forget. It is a great contribution to us that she carried alone this great culture for us in the family.

I am very grateful about my weaving. When I feel lonely wishing I had my parents or my younger sister around, I always sit down to my weaving and it's like my mother is still there with me and I remember all the stories and things she taught me making me feel better. I have a very special and close relationship with my loom and all the tools I use. It is this way in the Navajo way of life. You have to respect all things you use for your daily living.

My mother used to tell me not to forget all the things she taught me. She said, "Keep the spindle and carders in your hand. Don't ever store them away. Someday you will live on it. You will need it in your living way." My father used to tell me, "You will be the one to tell the stories of The Long Walk, so they won't be forgotten." I look back over my life and I am happy. For I have kept my promises to my mother and my father that I would never set aside what a great culture they taught me.

—*Tiana Bighorse*

From Fleece to Yarn 1

. . . the spinning song says the spindle shaft is made of turquoise and the whorl of white shell. The turquoise stands for male and the white shell is female. The song always talks about the four directions and the four sacred mountains.

—Navajo weaver, Tuba City

There is a sense of sameness in a traditional Navajo woman's life: the vastness of time immersed in subsistence. Gather wood. Tend fire. Feed children. Daily tasks carried out in the face of unrelenting heat, sandblasting winds, severe winters. Without the amenities most urban Americans take for granted, basics are full-time pursuits.

Given the demands of daily life and the slowness of the weaving process—the way all aspects of the craft require tending—it is a miracle that Navajo rugs exist at all.

First you must raise the sheep. Herd them across the sparsely vegetated, semi-desert land in search of forage. On alternate days, you must get the flock to water—a scarcity in the great Southwest. The sheep are hardy; you value them for the way they survive and still produce meat. The wool, poor. But considering the conditions under which it comes to be, fleece is a gift.

Your hands are strong for shearing. There is no electricity at the sheep camp so you sharpen and resharpen handshears throughout the day. Besides, electric shears cannot cut through the wind-embedded grit deep within the fleece. Relatives join together for a workday. Hand shearing is slow, yet the gathering is congenial; humor and mutton stew mellow the job.

Now you comb the fleece to prepare it for spinning. Use tow cards—handled wooden combs with metal teeth. Remove stickers and debris by hand. Interaction with the wool is direct and intimate.

Spinning is by shaft and whorl—no mechanized wheel. You spin carded fibers lightly, pull them out to the right size for yarn, then respin. You handle each inch of yarn again and again. Be patient. The wool from the Navajo sheep is short and kinky; spinning an even yarn comes with years of practice.

Grace Homer, shearing sheep.

Don't save wool from year to year because moths come after a year.

Sometimes they get into the warp if it's in a ball and chew right through.

Then when you string the loom, the warp keeps breaking.

—Tiana Bighorse, Tuba City

Learning to Card

Gusts picked at the edges of the silted earth, first gently, then with growing vigor, until a mauve haze obscured the flat sageland before me. I urged my son to hurry. In his small hand he clenched a worn food card. On the back a young Navajo man two days before had drawn an intricate map to his mother's hogan. His mother, a weaver.

Shawn, six, was my moral support, a help in countering my failing resolve. I had been on reservation less than a week. There were at least two years ahead during which to leisurely find a weaver. Learning Navajo weaving couldn't require two years of motivated, concerted effort. I could go next week. . . .

I headed the car down the road.

Finding a weaver had not been easy. The terse traders, Navajo rugs piled about them, knew of none. The urbane doctor's wives, unventuring in their year of stay, knew of none. My husband, Jack, home from his first day at the new hospital, had encountered none.

As we turned onto the rutted road at the trading post, the cards to comb the wool bounced beside me and I steadied them. Already they were looking used. Two days before, Jack, home for lunch amidst packing boxes, had listened sympathetically to my frustration in finding a weaver. When he left for the hospital, I lay down for a nap, but no sooner had I closed my eyes when I heard him open the door again.

"I know you need a rest. But I know you'll like it even less if I go to work without telling you. There's a lady sitting in the brush herding sheep—and she's combing her wool!"

I hurried across sand and sage toward a distant figure bleached in noon-day glare. With mild curiosity she watched me. At close range her dark, bright eyes and rutted skin caused me to hesitate. I didn't speak Navajo; she probably didn't speak English. I settled beside her in the sun.

"Hello."

She spoke in Navajo and continued carding: wool on the left card, just the right amount; right card on top; a series of long combing motions; a quick double sliding push-pull.

She was carding with her back to her flock. Behind her I could see sheep grazing contentedly in prime Tuba City pasturage—Anglo doctors' lawns. Approximately every half hour she glanced about. "Surprised" at seeing the sheep nibbling in gardens, she jumped up and herded them back to the barren sagebrush and then resumed carding. While I watched, the sheep made their way back to greener grass. After two hours, she suddenly got up, flung a word melodically into the silence, and left. Her sheep with her.

Within minutes, I was on my way to the trading post to buy my own cards. Back home I positioned wool and cards precisely as I had seen her do. Comb. Grate. Mesh. She had turned her wool to silk, mine was now matted. I continued to practice. At the end of the day, sitting by a pile of jumbled wool rolls, I resolved to find a weaver to teach me.

Years before, as a foreign exchange student in Germany, I had sat on cobblestones and painted village scenes. Soon the local children discovered the artista. *Not long afterwards, parents came to get their kids—and peek at the painting. A conversation was initiated. Then a lunch invitation. Suddenly, there we were eating bratwurst and black bread.*

So maybe if I sat in the middle of town carding, someone would help me learn. All I needed was a good location and enough courage. Tuba City options were limited: two trading posts, an elementary school, a Dairy Queen, one gas station, and the laundromat.

The women do the laundry and the women do the weaving. I piled dirty clothes into the jeep, cards and wool on top. Half an hour later, laundry turning inside machines, I sat on the ground outside and began to card. Women and children took notice and stood near, forming a circle. No one said a word. Time went by. I began to realize Tuba City wasn't Beutelsbach.

No one pitied my clumsiness with the cards.

Card black and white together to make grey. Use as much white and as much black as you want to make the grey how light or dark you want it. Just card lightly. When you've carded all of it, take about ten cardings [rolags] in your hand and pull them apart into pieces. Mix all these pieces in one pile. Card them again. The grey won't be streaked.

—Tiana Bighorse, Tuba City

No matter how much difficulty I encountered, no one offered help. No advice. No words at all. Just a soft easy giggle occasionally rippling around the growing circle. There was nothing to do but continue. Intently. Completely. With singleness of mind.

Perhaps fifteen minutes later I looked up to face the silence. Women were now three deep about me. A black pickup was pulling to a stop at the edge of the crowd, a young man and woman were getting out. Slowly the woman came over and knelt beside me.

"What are you doing?"

It wasn't a positive, inquisitive "What are you doing?" Nor was it a negative, derogatory "What are you doing!" The inflection was neutral. Flat. Balanced just in between.

"I'm trying to card wool."

Dead silence.

Wrong answer! Could have said anything but that.

An inner dialogue filled in the unnerving space. I desperately wished someone would help me, so I said aloud, "I'm having a hard time."

Silence.

Self-evident. Words wasted on the obvious. Don't talk now till she does.

I began a new batch of wool, intent on match-

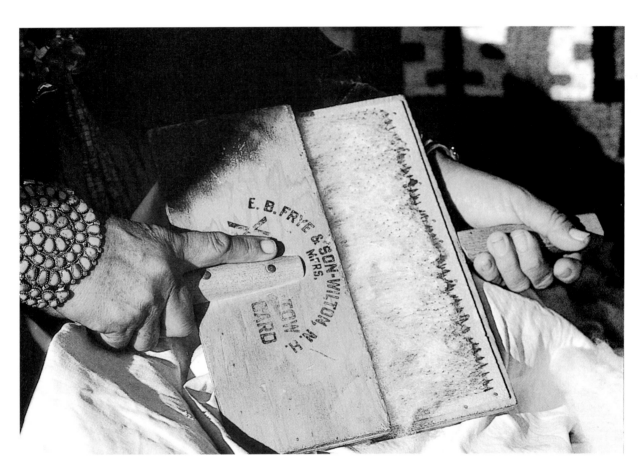

Tiana Bighorse, carding.

ing her reserve. I came to the end. Still she hadn't spoken. I laid another wool roll on the pile.

"Can you help me?"

Silence.

"Just keep carding."

I know, now, her answer was the best that could have been given—my mind knew the method; my hands had yet to refine pressure and rhythm. But that was not what I wanted to hear. I wanted real help: "You're holding the cards wrong. You're using too much pressure. Too much wool."

But the silence had been broken. And questions now bobbed up in various parts of the circle, then traveled in Navajo around the perimeter. When they came to the young woman, she translated.

"They want to know where you get your wool."

"It's my mother's sheep," I answered, knowing that with the Navajo, sheep belong to the women. "From California." Translation into Navajo. Hands reaching to feel "California wool." Again, indistinguishable clicks and stops coming the course of the circle.

"What color is it?" Lips pointed toward the dirty wool before me. The question was odd to me. I answered the obvious.

"It's white." Then clarified, "I haven't washed it yet." The translation went around but quickly came back.

"They think it's grey; they can't believe it's white."

I looked at my dirty white wool. Mixed with black California soil, it was grey. Maybe the Navajo white wool, mixed with red Arizona soil, would be pink. I shared the thought. Many hands reached into the bag and my mother's sheep disappeared into the circle.

The next question came quickly.

"They want to know who's training you."

The wording was strange to me, but the question was in the right place. I took my time with the answer. There was a beauty in not having to blurt out the first thing that came to mind. "Nobody. . . . Yesterday I watched an old lady carding in the sagebrush. . . . I'd like to learn more. . . ."

Stillness. Stillness. Unrelenting stillness.

"Do you know anyone who could teach me?"

As soon as I heard my own words, I chided myself. I had now asked twice. I returned to carding. In the time it took to process three more wool rolls, the woman from the pickup began to speak.

"My mother-in-law weaves." My heart pounded hopefully. "She's a good weaver." Another wool-roll later. "She sells her rugs at the

The women just let the wool stand in the sun. They pick a place where there is good sand. Every day they just go over and pick up the wool and shake it a little. Then they turn it over and lay it back down. The wind blows sand into it and the sun makes the oil soft and the sand absorbs the oil. They say it takes the strength out if you use soap.

—Navajo weaver, Tuba City

Cameron Trading Post."

"Would she teach me?"

"You ask her. She speaks good English."

Her husband drew the map on the back of a food card. The woman, Clara, assured me I could come any time. I loaded the now very clean, wet clothes, the worn food card, and what was left of Mom's wool in the back of the jeep. I drove off with one of the first headaches of my life.

Later, when I did formally ask Tiana Bighorse if she would teach me, her reply was to the point.

"How long do you have to learn?"

I would be in Tuba City two years. There seemed no better answer. But I waited for what I thought to be an appropriate time, then confidently said:

"Two years." Her expression clouded and I hastily added, "Will that be enough?"

She shifted her eyes. Downward, then back at me.

"Perhaps."

Tiana Bighorse, spinning.

The Spinning Song is generally sung at the puberty rites or ceremony for the young girls who have reached the age of womanhood. It is said that if one knows this song, all wealth, riches, and good blessings will be bestowed upon her.

—Tribal chairman, Window Rock

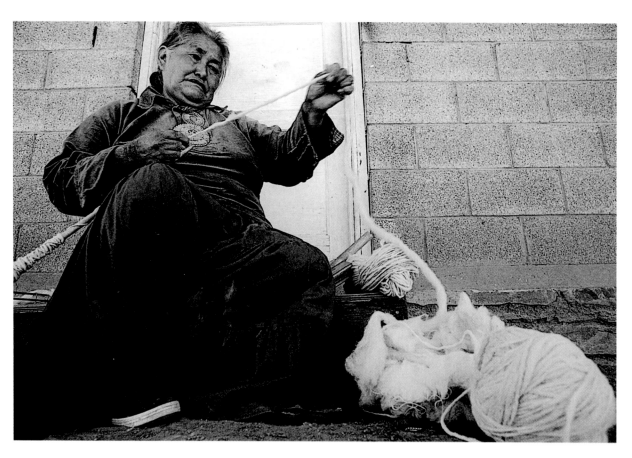

Grace Homer, spinning.

Learning to Spin

The simple secret to spinning is practice. Once mastered, it is relaxing. Soothing. Productive. Easily done while visiting with friends or sitting alone by a river. Meditative, it occupies the hands; lets the mind take flight.

One summer my mother and I vacationed along the McKensie River in Oregon. She wanted to learn to spin. So we made her a spindle from things on hand and began at once. Several times that week, when her yarns broke and her spindle fell, she remarked she might be no good at spinning. Might never be able to learn. I told her what one Navajo weaver told me. "You can't complain until after the tenth skein."

A few weeks after Mom returned home. I received a package in the mail—yarn and a simple note: "Skein #1." It looked pretty nubby; in some places it was actually discontinuous. The next skein, #3, arrived several weeks later and looked considerably better. Skein #8 looked even and confident. I never got another. In their later years, Dad joked that Mom loved spinning so much, she would pay people just to let her teach them.

The spindle

When I wanted to learn to spin, I asked Tiana Bighorse at which trading post I could get a spindle. And how to pick out a good one. She said, "We make our own."

That day she helped me make my first spindle. We crafted the shaft from a dowel she had on hand. Then she gave me a Quaker Oats box top to trace onto a pine board as pattern for the whorl. I cut out the wooden circle, rasped a bevel all around, and sanded it smooth. I have spun on many spindles since. But the one I made that day under her guidance is still my favorite.

The Navajo spindle is made of two pieces of wood—a tapered shaft and a round flat whorl

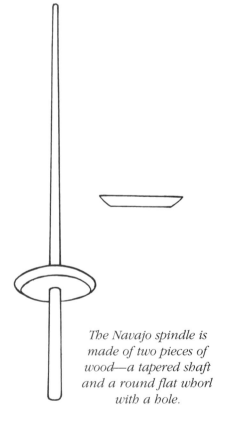

The Navajo spindle is made of two pieces of wood—a tapered shaft and a round flat whorl with a hole.

with a hole. The whorl slips onto the shaft and rests about two-thirds of the way down. It is important to understand the nuances of this simple spindle. The shaft must be very straight. Its length depends on where you will be sitting as you spin. If you sit on a chair, a shaft about 33 inches (84 cm) long works well. (Some Navajo weavers have different sizes of spindles, including one with a shorter shaft to be used when sitting on the ground or the floor.) The whorl must be very round to prevent wobble and made of lightweight wood such as pine so the spindle can be quickly started and stopped. A heavy hardwood whorl keeps spinning longer, but is unwieldy to work with.

Spinning motions

There are two spinning motions, used separately and in combination. Practice them both with the spindle only, no wool. The following directions are for spinning right-handed. Navajo weavers who are left-handed sometimes spin this way, too; less frequently, they reverse the entire process.

Sit in an upright, armless chair on rug or dirt. (Spindles slide and fall easily on slick floor surfaces.) Position your right foot back slightly and your left foot out comfortably in front of you, so your right knee is a bit higher than your left.

Fingertip twirl

Hold the top of the spindle in your right hand alongside your right leg, halfway between your knee and thigh. Hold the tip of the spindle between your thumb and two fingertips. Snap your middle finger sharply across the back of the shaft to start the spindle into motion. Let the spindle spin clockwise in the opening between your thumb and index finger. Stop the spindle by pressing it with your middle finger or let it gradually come to a stop by itself. Practice this many times.

At first the spindle may frantically wobble side to side. Steady it by rotating the circle formed by your thumb and index finger slightly toward you. Practice until the spindle spins contentedly, calmly, in balance.

Try starting the spindle in various positions: vertical, slanting toward you, slanting away from you. Start in one position and move it to another while it keeps spinning. Move it around. Practice until you can do this easily.

Vary the braking speeds. Start the spindle and stop it immediately. Start it, move it around while it continues to spin, bring it slowly to a rest. Vary the routine while practicing.

Sustained spin

With the base of the shaft on the floor about 12 to 16 inches (30 to 41 cm) to the right of your heel, rest the top of the spindle shaft against your right leg. Cradle the shaft loosely in your right hand, palm on top, thumb below. In proper position, you can feel your kneecap with your fingertips.

Stroke the spindle into motion by pressing the shaft against your leg and drawing your palm toward you. When you feel the shaft just pass your fingertips, scoop it into the crook of your thumb, lift it back to the original position, and stroke it toward you again. Scoop, stroke. Scoop, stroke. Scoop, stroke. When you are doing this correctly, the spindle will continue twirling in the same (clockwise) direction while being lifted back to its starting position by the knee cap.

Keep practicing the sustained spin until you get used to the feel of the scoop-stroke. See how many times you can stroke it before losing control. At first you may be able to do it only three or four times before it falls off your leg. Continue to practice, noting the pressure you are applying with all your fingers. Broad contact from all your fingers creates a steady, controlled spin.

The combination:
fingertip twirl to sustained spin

With the spindle upright, snap it into motion with your fingertips and immediately bring it to your knee (with the shaft still spinning in the crook of your thumb). Stroke it toward you using the sustained spin. Once the spindle passes your fingertips, scoop it back to the original position and stroke it toward you again. The rhythm is: fingertip twirl, stroke, scoop-stroke, scoop-stroke, scoop-stroke. The spinning is smooth, continuous, steady. Practice the combination until the two motions work as one.

When the fingertip twirl and sustained spin feel comfortable alone and together, you are ready to proceed. When I learned to spin from Tiana, I simply watched her and did what she did. There was no talking. The Navajo word for "teach" is the same word as "show".

Transforming Carded Wool into Yarn

During carding, wool assumes the shape of a loose roll or rolag. Navajo weavers usually prepare a supply of rolags before starting to spin.

Attaching the first rolag to the spindle

Attaching a rolag securely to the spindle is the first step in spinning.

1. Insert the tip of the spindle shaft about 2 inches (5 cm) from the end of the rolag.

2. Fold the end of the rolag back and, at the shaft, pinch all the fibers between your left thumb and index finger.

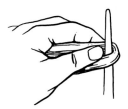

3. With your right hand, rotate the spindle three times end for end (top toward you, bottom away from you) to create a tight, strong twist between the shaft and your fingers. The section of the rolag that tightly wraps around the spindle forms the attachments. Transfer the shaft and attachment to your right hand, maintaining the twist.

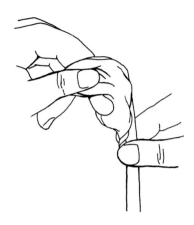

Be sure to allow slack between jerks so that the twist will distribute itself along the rolag before the next jerk. Releasing tension between jerks is the secret of creating uniform yarn. As you jerk and release, watch how the twists cluster where the rolag is thinnest, thereby strengthening these thin places. Watch also how the thick places shun the twist, which leaves them vulnerable to being pulled out with the next jerk.

When pulling out the yarn, the rhythm is: Jerk, release. Jerk, release. Getting the right amount of spin is important. If you don't have enough spin, the rolag will break; if you have too much, it won't pull out. Regulate your spin so that when you jerk-release, the fibers pull out smoothly and evenly. The section of rolag being pulled out approximately doubles in length.

4. Grasp the rolag with your left hand, about 5 inches (13 cm) from the spindle. Lift the rolag directly above the tip of shaft, allowing slack.

   The rolag should not be taut. With your right hand, let go of the twist and give the spindle a fingertip twirl. Let the rolag coils slip off the tip three to four times.

5. With your right hand, hold the spindle vertically, shaft on floor. Hold the attachment with your thumb and index finger to make sure it doesn't slip off the tip. With your left hand, gently pull the rolag away from the spindle using short jerking motions. Do not let go of the rolag or of the attachment, or the rolag will untwist and break.

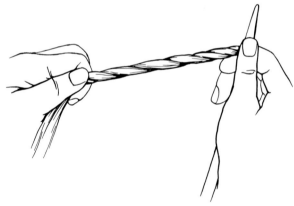

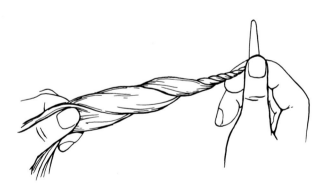

6. When your hands are almost 11 inches (28 cm) apart, with your right hand, push the attachment 5 inches (13 cm) down the shaft to secure a better hold. Spin the 11-inch (28-cm) section of rolag by holding it loosely above the tip of the shaft. After twirling the spindle with your fingertips, let the rolag coils slip over the tip. Slide the attachment further down the shaft.

Wind the spun yarn onto the shaft using the fingertip twirl. Place the junction between your spun yarn and unspun rolag about 1 inch (2.5 cm) below the tip, and hold it there with your right hand.

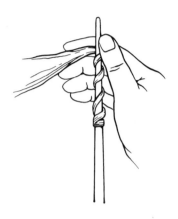

The first rolag is now attached to the spindle. Continue spinning until you've spun enough yarn to push the attachment all the way down to the whorl. Then you'll be ready to settle into the rhythm of spinning.

If you can't master the process of attaching a rolag, skip this step for now and come back to it after you've learned to spin. To begin, simply tie an arm's length of commercial yarn above the whorl and wind it up the shaft (turning the spindle clockwise). Then tie the yarn to one end of a rolag and wind the join around the shaft, about 1 inch (2.5 cm) below the tip.

Spinning

There are five steps in the process of spinning rolags into yarn:

Step 1. Use the fingertip twirl to twist and strengthen a section of the rolag.

With your right hand, pinch the junction between the spun and unspun rolag, just below the shaft tip. With your left hand, hold the end of the rolag loosely above the shaft tip. Allow plenty of slack. With your right hand, give the spindle a fingertip twirl. With practice, you'll learn how to twist the rolag just enough, but not too much. If you don't twist it enough, the rolag pulls apart. If you twist it too much, it's hard to pull out.

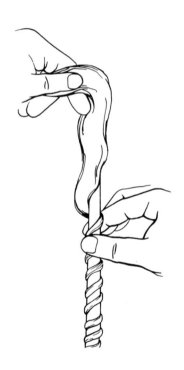

Step 2. Jerk-release the twisted section to thin it and even it out.

With your right hand, hold the spindle vertically on the floor and pinch the yarn against the spindle tip. With your left hand, pull the rolag out to a uniform thickness (as in the drawing at right on page 25). Jerk-release. Jerk-release.

Violet Chee at Hubbell Trading Post, spinning.

As you tug the rolag, it will get longer. Give the spindle a fingertip twirl to add more twist whenever it feels like the rolag is pulling out too easily and might be about to break. When the rolag exceeds your reach, move your left hand closer to the spindle, letting the rest of the rolag hang free. Add more twist as necessary, and jerk-release until the section of rolag between your hands is the right thickness for the yarn you want to make.

If you're having trouble with slubs or thick spots, hold the yarn on both sides of the problem area with your fingers about 3 inches (7.5 cm) apart. Untwist the yarn by rotating your right hand away and your left hand toward you.

Remove the slub or sticker if necessary. Then with the heels of your hands braced against each other, pull out that section of the yarn. (This "controlled pull," with hands braced together to give more control and leverage, is how weavers break weft at the loom to create wisp ends.) Don't worry too much about thick and thin areas. They will be less apparent when the yarn is washed and set. The uniformity of your yarns will increase with spinning experience.

To learn to spin, just spin. Get in touch with the rhythm. The final goal is uniformity, but the immediate goal is achieving continuous yarn.

Step 3. Use the fingertip twirl/sustained spin to spin the thinned section into yarn.

Turn the palm of your left hand upward. Now touch the tips of your left thumb and index and middle fingers together very lightly, forming a triangular hole. This hole is your spinning orifice.

Unwind some yarn from the spindle and rewind it so that the junction between the spun yarn and the unspun rolag is about 4 inches (10 cm) below the tip of the shaft. Position the junction within the spinning orifice of your left hand.

In one continuous action, set the spindle in motion with a fingertip twirl/sustained spin. Then start sliding your left hand back along the rolag at a slow constant rate. As the rolag flows through your left hand, the twist runs about an inch or so in front of it. You are literally spinning each inch of your yarn. If, while spinning, you feel an occasional slub or sticker with your left hand, stop and remove it, then continue spinning.

Lily Nez in her hogan, spinning.

One day when Tiana was showing me how to spin, I asked, "How do you know how thick to spin the yarn?" She answered quietly, "Your hand knows."

How much you should spin the yarn depends on its thickness, the length of the wool fibers (shorter fibers need more spin than long ones do), and its intended use. Navajo weavers spin their weft yarn somewhat softly, which preserves its elasticity, helps it pack well, and keeps rug edges from pulling in. Their warp yarn is very tightly spun.

Beginning spinners almost always overspin their yarn, often because they are trying to spin a uniform yarn and think they can thin down thick areas by spinning them tightly. Not so. The extra twist always accumulates in the thin sections. The time to create uniformity is not when you're spinning the yarn, but when pulling out the rolag and refining the problem areas. When spinning, you should concentrate on spinning the already uniform yarn rhythmically and at a constant rate.

Step 4. Wind the yarn onto the spindle with the fingertip twirl.

When you've spun almost an arm's length of yarn, pinch the junction between the spun yarn and the unspun rolag with your left hand. Don't let go. Slant the spindle away from you and to your right. Pull back with your left hand to undo the yarn that's wrapped around the shaft; let the spindle spin freely in a hole formed by the index finger and thumb of the right hand until the yarn is pulled out. Now, with the spindle slanting well away from you, use the fingertip twirl to wind the yarn into a neat cone, starting against the whorl. The cone will keep the spindle balanced.

When the remaining yarn is a little longer than the exposed shaft, wind the yarn up the shaft so it ends up with the junction of spun and unspun rolag about 1 inch (2.5 cm) below the tip. You may need to do this several times to get it right. In time it will come naturally.

Step 5. When the rolag is almost entirely spun, join on another rolag with the fingertip twirl.

Repeat the previous steps, twisting and pulling the rolag and winding on the yarn, until you are about 3 inches (7.5 cm) from the end of the rolag. Then wind the yarn onto the spindle, wrapping it up the shaft so that the tail end is about 1 inch (2.5 cm) below the tip, ready to connect with the next rolag. Pull on the fibers to loosen the tail end, making it flat and fluffy. Do the same with the end of the new rolag. Overlap the two fluffy ends about 3 inches (7.5 cm). Roll a third of this join toward you and a third away from you. Brace your hands on each other as for a controlled pull to thin the join and to help the fibers stick together.

Spin the join into yarn by drawing it through your spinning orifice while twirling the spindle. Wind the spun join onto the shaft to secure it. Then spin the rest of the rolag.

Most Navajo weavers today spin each carded rolag completely—that is, as fine as they want it—before attaching the next rolag. In the old days, some women joined many rolags together, forming a loose strand called roving, and then spun the entire roving two to five times—each time with increasing fineness. One woman told me that this was how she did it when she was a child herding sheep; she could easily carry a day's work with her. Some weavers still spin warp yarn this way, because it must be very fine and very tight.

Skeining Yarn off the Spindle

When the spindle is full, wind the yarn off into a skein. Here's the Navajo way:

Remove your right shoe and cross your right leg over the left. Grasp the end of the yarn with your left hand, palm up, yarn end to the left. With your right hand, loosely hold the spindle shaft below the whorl. Tuck the bottom tip of the shaft under your right forearm so the spindle can rotate freely. Reach down and pass the spindle behind your foot from right to left, and bring the yarn up to your left hand. You have made one counterclockwise loop.

Secure the loop by tying the two pieces of yarn in your left hand with a square knot. The yarn will reverse—that is, it will come out on the left of the square knot ready to circle your foot again in a clockwise direction.

Hold the loop taut and wind the rest of the yarn off the spindle, circling clockwise, working from hand to foot and back again. From hand to foot, let the spindle roll down taut loops. From foot to hand, let spindle rotate freely, the bottom tip of the shaft still tucked beneath your forearm.

When all the yarn has been wound off, don't let go of the tension. Keep the skein under tension between your left hand and right foot. Hold the tail end of the yarn in your right hand and rotate the skein until your hands are about 15 inches (38 cm) apart. Transfer the tail end from your right hand to your left hand, letting

My hands are not strong enough to card very well. My fingers are not swift enough to spin very well. But my heart knows perfectly how it is done.

—Ann Clark, *Little Herder in the Autumn*

Weaver with Navajo spindle.

Now in those days, songs were very important. You sang a song to explain everything you were doing. People didn't talk so much. They even prayed with songs. They sang to Father Sky and Mother Earth, to the rain clouds and the corn spirits, to the Turquoise Goddess, and to all the animals. They sang songs to each other. When you sang a song you put all the power of your heart in it, and it was a holy thing.

—Margaret Schevill Link, *The Pollen Path*

it double back on itself into a two-ply yarn. Loosely wrap this length of two-ply around the skein, right where you are holding it in your left hand. Then tie it to itself with a square knot. Your skein now has a handle, by which you can hold the skein while washing or dyeing it, and which keeps the yarn in its proper orientation.

With your right hand, lift the skein off your foot. Keep it stretched between your hands and snap or jerk it a few times. Give it several twists by turning its right end toward you and its left end away. Then fold the skein in half and let it relax so that the doubled skein twists back on itself. Slide the left end of the skein (with its handle) through the end held in your right hand. The twisted skein is ready to store.

Washing the Skein

When you are ready to wash it, undo the twisted skein and shake it out, holding onto the handle. Submerge the skein in warm soapy water, squeezing water through the yarn several times until the yarn is clean. Transfer the skein to warm rinse water and gently squeeze it again. Repeat the rinsing process until the rinse water is clear. The skein is now ready for dyeing.

Whether the skein has just been washed or has also been dyed, you need to set the spin while the yarn is wet. Hang the skein anywhere it can drip (outdoors or indoors over the bathtub). Place a wooden weight (a piece of two-by-four, for example) through the bottom of the skein to keep it from kinking or snarling

I have to get lots of wood for the winter. It takes about twenty pickup loads for the whole winter for us. It always takes more if there is a weaver. Sometimes my wife makes a fire in the loom hogan and she weaves a lot. Sometimes she makes it in the bedroom. Then there is always extra things she needs wood for. Fire to dye the wool. Fire to wash it.

—Husband of Navajo weaver, Shonto

and to distribute the twist evenly on each strand. When the skein is completely dry, retwist it as before or loop it over the back of a chair and wind the yarn into a ball.

Spinning Warp

Warp yarn must be strong and resistant to abrasion, so it must be spun tightly. Use your best wool; long fiber is better than short. Warp can not be washed after spinning, so the fleece must be clean prior to carding.

Spin warp only after you can spin a good weft yarn and make joins between rolags that hold well. Until then, I recommend purchasing a strong, abrasion-resistant commercial warp yarn that has been plied to hold it flat, rather than using the traditional high-twist singles yarn.

Spin warp yarn as you do weft, except much thinner and much tighter. Move your left-hand spinning orifice very slowly along the yarn while the right hand maintains the sustained spin. To prevent kinking, keep the warp yarn under tension while spinning it and while winding it tightly onto the spindle.

Try to wind warp yarn into a perfect cone on the spindle. Wind it tightly and as low as possible—right on top of the whorl. Because warp is spun more tightly than weft, it is denser. You can wind four times as much warp yarn onto the spindle as you can weft. That extra weight makes it more important to wind the yarn carefully into a firm, neat cone; the spindle must be well balanced to spin well.

When the spindle is full, wind warp yarn tightly into a ball, wrapping it around an old thread spool, a rock, or a rolled piece of cardboard. Position the spindle so it is supported and can rotate freely (for example, you could lay the spindle on the arms of a slat-back chair

Twisted skein.

and feed the warp through the chair back). Keep dipping your hand in water to moisten the yarn as you wind the ball. Wind it tightly, straightening out any kinks.

When you're done, let the ball dry thoroughly. When the ball is dry and the spin is set—that is, when you can unwind a length of yarn and it stays flat without kinking—the warp is ready to use.

If you don't moisten the warp enough as you wind it into the ball, it will never lie flat. But if you add too much moisture the yarn will take too long to dry or will mold. The Navajo warp-making process is especially well suited to the dry climate of the Southwest, where yarn dries well even when in a tight ball, and stays dry (and flat) once it is woven into a rug.

This is not always the case. When I was restoring Navajo rugs, clients brought me textiles that had been housed in humid climates. They complained that the textiles had "shrunk" or "shriveled." Indeed, they rippled quite irregularly. The finer the tapestry, the worse it was! I finally determined that Navajo warp, with its twist set in a dry climate, can rehydrate in a moist climate and kink up, causing extremely strong contraction that can literally ruffle a very fine tapestry.

Notes on Navajo Dyes 2

When my mother goes to get some plants for her wool, she always takes her corn pollen pouch. Then when she gets to where the plants grow, she sprinkles them with the corn pollen and says sort of a prayer that means that they will make good colors and that they will grow again next year. Then she takes them. But if I go out there and get some, they just don't make good colors at all.

—Navajo weaver, Shonto

Dyeing the wool is next. You trek across the arid land. Hunt down certain roots and leaves and flowers. You think to yourself how well the plants do to survive—let alone produce evocative color. Not unlike your sheep gifting wool. Not unlike weavers creating beauty.

Sometimes the gathering is easy, as with the rabbitbrush that yields bright yellow, murky ochre, and yellow green. Sometimes the gathering is almost impossible, as with the mountain mahogany that grows at high elevations. The roots, seeking moisture, penetrate rock crevices. The roots release the prized deep-rust dye, so hacking with pick and shovel is slowly rewarded.

Sometimes you use chemical mordants to strengthen or change plant colors. Not alum from the corner drugstore, but alum from the alkaline washes that evaporate and yield the valued crystals. Or ashes of juniper boughs. Or galls from the oak.

There is real excitement in anticipating that the loom will bloom, but first you must know which plants to use, where to go, and you have yet to haul the water to wash the wool and boil the dye. Each phase is a quest, and many quests yield but a part. Be patient. In time, your skeins of yarn will vibrate with glowing color.

Green Dye Story

1968–1971: I'm living in Tuba City, Arizona, on the Navajo reservation and wanting to dye yarn green the way Navajo weavers do—using only what is at hand. No tin or other commercial mordants. So I ask various Navajo weavers how they make green. They tell me. I try it just as they say, but I always get yellow. I try rabbitbrush, juniper, owl's claw, sunflower, bitterball, mistletoe, Russian thistle, sagebrush, wild holly, Navajo tea, lichen, and others. On the gas stove in my kitchen I rotate enamel, aluminum, and iron pots. I vary the mordants: raw alum, cedar ashes, roots high in tannin. I keep exacting notes. Lemon, straw, gold, ochre—every time, yellow. For six years I record 117 unsuccessful attempts to make green. I conclude that weavers have the right to guard their precious secrets.

1971–1974: I am living in Gallup, New Mexico, teaching at the University of New Mexico, Gallup branch: weaving, spinning, carding, and dyeing. I have more Navajo students than Anglo. The class meets weekly to identify plants; later, students gather dyestuffs growing around their homes and dye with them; next class we compare colors and trade samples. One Navajo student complains that true yellow is difficult to get—hers always comes out green. I consider. Perhaps minerals in the water make green? Or minerals in the soil the plant grows in?

I am visiting my friend, Tiana Bighorse, in Tuba City. She has just finished a rug with a green border. She tells me she used to'iishįįhii, *but any yellow flower will do. I insist all yellow flowers make yellow; I've tried lots of them. She looks puzzled. No, they make green. We agree: I will bring her the plant and my water; she will show me. The next day, Tiana stuffs the plant materials I bring her in a handy nearby bucket, fills it three quarters full with my water, sets it in the fire to heat. Three hours later, deep green dye bubbles effortlessly in the pot.*

The color is in the bucket!

She has an extra one and gives it to me!

Back home I try the plants that failed before. All of them work. Everything that comes out of the bucket is green. I search out books with photos of Navajo weavers dyeing. Arizona Highways *magazine. John Running photographs. Invariably there's a heavy black bucket in the picture that looks like mine. Where do weavers get their black buckets? I ask around. Many years ago Tuba City Hospital threw out a bunch of old government-issue mop buckets. They work good in the open fire, so weavers like them for dyeing. Never thought about what they do to the color.*

I want to know what's in the bucket to turn dye

Tiana Bighorse, dyeing.

Making gad díílid díí *[cedar ashes]*

Build fire on non-windy day

Put grate or screen over collecting pot

Hold cedar bough over fire until ashes are ready to fall

Set on screen and leave alone, ashes will fall through

Repeat until have enough ashes

You can collect a lot of cedar boughs at one time and use these fresh or

dried for making ashes.

—Navajo weaver, Shonto

green. I ask a metal worker in Gallup. He puts a grinder to it, watches it spark. Says it's a kind of steel; impossible to tell what kind—too many possibilities. Probably soldered with lead, he adds. From a back corner he brings out a hunk of spring steel and a lump of lead. "See if you can make green dye in an enamel pot with these."

I take them home; they work the same as the bucket. That's how I come by the alchemical touchstone that transforms yellow into green.

Observations on Colorfastness

While learning to dye wool, I talked to lots of Navajo weavers and tried what they suggested. For each experiment, I recorded date, plant, location acquired, whether the plant was fresh or dried, the interval between gathering and using, the type of dyepot (enamel, aluminum, iron, copper, tin, other), fleece type, plant/water ratio, soaking and boiling times, straining method, mordant if any, simmering time, setting time, rinsing, and other observations.

Later I wove yarns dyed with various plants into a long sampler. Then I exposed one side to light for five years. I noted the color differences between the sides to determine the colorfastness. Here's what the sampler experiment suggests:

The greatest permanence of deep colors comes from plants high in tannic acid: Mormon tea, wild carrot, cedar (bark, berries, and mistletoe), walnut, and cliff rose. Also, rabbitbrush and sagebrush produce lasting yellows.

Natural fleece colors, with the exception of black/brown, are extremely colorfast.

Colors that use soda as mordant fade more than those that use other mordants.

All colors from fruits and berries, which originally were bright and desirable hues, fade beyond usefulness.

There is no evident difference in color retention between wool and mohair.

Basic Dyeing Directions

If you use fresh plants, do not soak them. If you use dried plants, soak them overnight. If the plant material is hard (roots, bark, and hulls, for example), pound it first.

The type of pot you use depends on the plants you will work with, as described in each recipe below. Iron and aluminum pots create duller shades; steel and lead objects can also be added to the dyebaths.

Step 1. Fill the pot with the plant and water until it is three quarters full. Boil the plant material for one to two hours and remove it from the dye bath.

Step 2. Slowly add the appropriate mordant while stirring, to prevent a foaming overflow. Boil for ten minutes.

Step 3. Immerse a clean skein of yarn in a pot of warm water. Heat until the water is very hot. Squeeze the skein gently and transfer it immediately to the dye bath.

Step 4. Simmer the yarn for at least 1 hour. Do not boil.

Step 5. Remove the pot from the heat and let the yarn cool in the dyebath. Leaving the yarn in the dyebath overnight will intensify or deepen some colors.

Step 6. Remove the yarn from the dyebath. Rinse the skein well and hang it to dry.

Mordanting the Navajo Way

Navajo dyeing reflects harmony with nature. No chemical mordants are used—only those that occur naturally. Mordants are added directly to the dyebath, so the process has appealing immediacy and simplicity.

The mordants

Quantities of mordant are based on the use of a 3-gallon (10- to 12-liter) pot.

Raw alum: An alkaline crystal-like substance found in washes or other areas of recent water evaporation. Add 1/4 cup (60 ml) directly to dyebath, boil 10 minutes. (Substitution with similar results: Add 1 tablespoon (15 ml) of aluminum potassium alum to the dyebath.)

Cedar ashes: Ashes prepared from the Rocky Mountain juniper (*juniperus monosperma*), which Navajo weavers call "cedar."

Whenever I see certain plants that make certain dyes, I always take them and use them. My mother always tells me that the plants are put there for the Navajo to use. If we don't use them, then the gods will just think that nobody needs them and after a while there aren't any to use.

—Tiana Bighorse, Tuba City

Collect juniper branch tips about 1 foot (30 cm) long. Build an outdoor fire on a windless day. Set fire to each branch and lay it on a grill with a container beneath to catch the ashes. To dye 1/4 pound (113 g) of yarn you will usually need 1/4 cup (60 ml) of ashes. Store surplus ashes for future use. To make the mordant, add the juniper ashes to twice the amount of boiling water, stir, and strain. (Substitution with similar results: Ashes from other hardwood.)

Salt: Add directly to the dyebath without straining.

Soda and baking powder: Similar to raw alum. Add 1 tablespoon (15 ml) directly to dyebath without straining.

The Dyeing Process

Below are guidelines and recipes for creating dyes with several plants used by Navajo weavers. The Latin and Navajo names for the plants follow the English name.

Twiggy flowering plants

Rabbitbrush (Chrysothamnus graveolens) (k'iiłtsoiitsoh): Rabbitbrush is easy to collect, so it is a good plant to experiment with using different mordants and pots. It can be used year round. The yellow color is brightest during late summer bloom. The dye is extremely colorfast. The various species of this clumpy shrub grow abundantly up to 5 feet (1.5 m) tall at elevations below 7000 feet (2134 m). The plant is especially common along highways where runoff increases moisture. The leaves are long, thin, and of uniform width.

Part used: Flowers, twigs, leaves.

Procedure: Fill 3-gallon (10- to 12-liter) enamel pot with packed rabbitbrush clippings. Add water until the pot is three quarters full. Boil the plant material one hour and then remove it. Depending on the color you want, add the mordant listed below. Add 1/4 pound (113 g) of wet, hot yarn. Simmer the yarn for

42

Rabbitbrush, an easy-to-gather source of yellows.

1/2 hour to create lighter tints, 1 to 3 hours for deeper shades. Rinse in water.

Mordants and notes:

For yellow: 1/4 cup (60 ml) raw alum (1 teaspoon [5 ml] of commercial alum), enamel pot. Boil 10 minutes.

For yellow orange: 1 tablespoon (15 ml) soda, enamel pot. Boil 10 minutes.

For ochres and mustards: Use aluminum pot.

For green: Use steel bucket (or steel/lead objects in enamel pot).

Other plants that use the same method

Sagebrush *(Artemesia tridentata)* (ts'ah): yellows, ochres, greens

Chamizo *(Atriplex canescens)* (diwózhiiłbei): greens, yellows

Mormon Tea *(Ephedra vividis)* (tł'oh azihii): tans

Mistletoe *(Phoradendron spp.)* (dahts'aa'): yellows, greens. Grows as a parasite in juniper trees. Appears from distance as dark clump. Easy to collect. One bath yields multiple dyeings.

Cliff Rose *(Cowania stanisburiana)* ('awééts'áál): golds, tan, brown

Barks, roots, and lichens

Wild carrot (Rumex hymenosepalus) (chąąt'inii): Do not confuse with Queen Anne's Lace *(Daucus carota)*. Wild carrot grows abundantly in sandy soil appropriate for their extensive root systems. They are "ghost" plants. They appear in the spring with fleshy, broad, dark green leaves, above which is a single-stemmed flower cluster. Almost overnight they are nowhere to be seen—a shriveled black shadow marks their spot. The foliage has withered and died. This is the time for gathering.

Wild carrots are high in tannic acid, so they require no mordant for colorfastness. Successive dyebaths yield continuing color.

Part used: Root. To collect the root, dig around the dried foliage, 1 to 2 feet (30 to 60 cm) deep. Gather new roots (bright orange when broken) and old "rotten" ones (last year's crop). Each yields a different color.

Use the roots fresh or dried. To dry, cut them into pieces and lay them in the sun for several days. Turn occasionally.

Procedure: If roots have been dried, soak them overnight. Cut fresh roots into pieces. Add four parts water to one part roots. Boil 1 to 2 hours and remove plant material. Strain. Add mordant for colors described below. Add wet, hot yarn. Simmer 1 hour. Rinse immediately or leave in pot overnight depending on depth of color you want.

Mordants and notes:

For gold or orange: Young roots (orange interior) in aluminum or enamel pot.

For burnt red orange: Young roots (orange interior) with soda and salt in aluminum pot.

For gold or mustard: Mature roots (yellow interior) in enamel pot.

For ochre or brown: Old roots (rotten) in aluminum or iron pot.

For dark brown: Old roots (rotten) with soda and salt in aluminum or iron pot.

Other plants that use the same method

Cedar *(Juniperus monosperma)* (gad): browns, tans, rusts

Oak galls and leaves *(Quercus gambeli)* (chéch'il): browns, tans, golds

Wild Holly roots *(Berbens fremontii)* (k'iiłtsoiitsoh): yellow

Alder *(Alnus tenufolia)* (k'ish): browns, tan to reddish

Lichen *(Parmelia molluscula)* (ni'hadlááad): orange, rust, gold

Grace Homer, with dyed fleece.

Scarce and sacred plants

We suggest that you do not use the following plants to make dyes. Some of them are considered sacred. For example, beeweed saved the Navajo people long ago from starvation; the Hopi use Wild Tea for ceremony. Other plants are simply scarce, or collecting kills them, or the dyes they produce are fugitive.

Mountain Mahogany *(Cercocarpus montanus)* (tse'ásdaazii)

Wild Tea *(Thelesperma gracile)* (ch'il gohwéhé)

Prickly Pear *(Opuntia polyacantha)* (hosh niteelí)

Indian Paintbrush *(Castilleja integre)* (dahyiitį́hídą́ą́')

Lupine *(Lupinus kingii)* ('azee' diilch'iłii)

Beeweed *(Cleome serrulata)* (waa')

Wild Carrot Story

One hot afternoon Tiana and I drive north of Tuba City for wild carrot. The color-bearing roots grow two feet beneath the sandy surface. We must dig deep.

We sort each root clump as we find it: young tubers yield a valued orange dye, old ones a mustard color, "rotten" ones, brown. Wild carrot contains tannic acid, so it is one of the most colorfast of the native dyes. Throughout the tiring work, my friend and I talk of the miracle of wild carrot: the colors of sweet melon, sacred squash, the setting sun—all from the same hole.

Before we push the dirt back in, we place a young, moist tuber in the bottom. "Here's to the next year."

Tiana and I need enough for the coming year, so we dig all afternoon until the car is filled and heat stroke threatens. Back at her hogan, I split the roots in preparation for drying. Then divide and stash our booty: mine in my jeep, hers under her bed.

Just as we sit down, I see a distant figure running toward us. It descends the mesa edge. Briskly covers the long, hot stretch of flat sageland to the hogan. Soon I recognize the old lady.

Once inside, she sniffs her way around the space. "Chąąt'inii halchin!" Peers into every crevice. "Chąąt'inii halchin!"

"She says she smells wild carrot." Tiana looks at me knowingly.

Her friend darts around the hogan. Checks behind the wood-burning stove. Ever so surely edges toward the bed. Moments later, down on hands and knees, she pulls out the dyestuffs we have just stashed. In no time at all, according to Navajo protocol, Tiana has divided up her cache of carrot to share with her clan relative.

Tools and Yarns 3

All tools which are used for weaving have to be well taken care of. Fork and other tools must never be used for scratching one's itch or as a toothpick. These tools represent rainbow and lightning [and] can be harmful when used for the wrong purpose.

—Navajo weaver, Gallup

Navajo weavers value their tools. Give them special care. Sometimes men make tools and sell them to the trading post. But weavers who take pride in, and derive pleasure from, the weaving process, do not buy trading-post tools. You make your own.

Walk the high elevation land among the Scrub Oak and Fendler. Quest the perfect branch. And curve. Carve and sand it into shape. Be patient. Soon it will be yours.

You already have a few battens and forks that were passed down from Mother and Grandmother. Old wooden implements, shiny, smooth, and deeply grooved with wear; they are among your greatest treasures.

There is power in a tool. To lend one is to give of your power. So, you do not leave your tools lying around to be used by just anyone.

And when you do lend one, it is only to a close and trusted friend. For to loan a tool is to gift energy and ideas.

The Set of Tools

A Navajo weaver's complete set of tools includes:

- Several battens, ranging in size from 1½ inches (4 cm) wide down to 1/4 inch (6 mm) wide or narrower.

- Two forks: one about 2 inches (5 cm) wide, the other about 1 inch (2.5 cm) wide

- An umbrella rib

- A sacking needle

- Two or three straight twigs with broken ends, to use as shuttles

47

The Tool Pouch

As you gather tools for your weaving, you will want to keep them together and safe. Navajo weavers often rip up an old pair of jeans and use one of the legs as a ready-made case. They just stitch the bottom together and tie the top with a cord or leather thong.

The Batten

The batten is a basic and cherished weaving tool. Its purpose is to separate the warp to allow a weft to pass through. Each batten has a slight curve on one end to ease its insertion between warps.

For your first project, start with two battens: one medium (1 inch [2.5 cm] wide) and one small (1/2 inch [1.25 cm] wide). You will use the medium batten for the first half of the weaving, and the smaller one as the weaving space gets tighter. You can purchase battens (see Sources of Information and Supplies), or make your own.

A good batten requires a special kind of hold a curve. If you are purchasing specialty wood, look for a heavy, oily tropical wood such as cocobolo, lignum vitae, or cordia. Avoid light or brittle woods such as ebony, walnut, teak, maple, and ash.

How to make a batten

When wandering through a forested area, look carefully for hardwood branches. You will need two: one that is about 1½ inches (4 cm) in diameter and one that is 3/4 inches (2 cm) in diameter. Both should have a straight section about 27 inches (69 cm) long ending in a slight curve.

Cut the branches to length—about 30 inches (76 cm). Now look at the shape and curve of each branch to determine which sides to flatten. The top and bottom edges should be quite straight; the left end should curve toward you. Remove the bark and rasp the back and front sides until the batten is about 3/8 inch (9 mm) thick.

Now, still holding the batten so that the left end curves toward you, shape the ends as

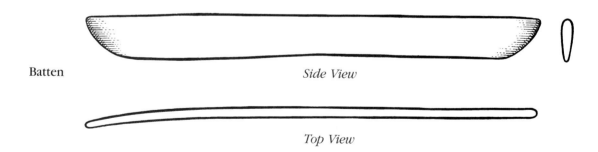

Batten

Side View

Top View

hardwood. Navajo weavers prize desert-grown oak—Scrub, Gambel, or Fendler—*(Quercus* spp.*) (chéch'il* or *tsitł'íz)*. These woods hold up over time and acquire a beautiful patina from handling and from rubbing against warp threads. Unlike eastern oak, they also take and shown above. The insertion end—the left end—is the most important. It should be "boat shaped"—that is, longer at the top. Now rasp the top edge to thin it a bit. Rasp the bottom edge, thinning it even more. Sand and oil the wood. Your battens are ready.

Don't use the batten for something other than weaving—like to spank the children, or to hit your husband, or to move something close that you can't reach. Because something happens to you so you can't weave as well. Sore back. Tired arms. Maybe that's what happened to those young girls who complain they get tired when they weave.

It's okay to use the batten in a ceremony.

—Tiana Bighorse, Tuba City

When a batten does not curve enough, Navajo weavers coat it liberally with mutton fat and bury it in wet sand with a heavy weight placed at the point where the curve should be, as shown below. After a week, it is curved enough.

Alternatively, coat the batten with oil. Bake it in an oven at 300°F (150°C). Slide the curved end 3 inches (7.5 cm) under a heavy weight (or a gap under a door) and raise the opposite end about 8 inches (20 cm). Let the wood cool. If the batten is still not curved enough, repeat the process and increase the lifting pressure. The right wood is essential. Good woods will hold the curve; brittle woods will break.

One method for shaping a batten.

Batten and fork in warp.

A weaver doesn't give her weaving tools up easily. One woman I knew used to be a really good weaver. And fast, too. And her husband had a good job. And maybe it was because of that, but she all of a sudden decided to give away all of her weaving tools—that she had no further use for them.

And she gave her spindle to one and her fork to another and she gave away her battens to everyone. And after that she began drinking. And we try to help her, but it doesn't work. One Christmas I told her I needed two small looms made, and she should make them, and it took her too long to make them. Two months, maybe. It was as though she just couldn't do it anymore.

They say the tools and the stories are just like your head, or your ideas, or your energy. That's why weavers are so hesitant to loan them to people, because they get the power from you.

—Navajo weaver, Tuba City

Fork pattern, actual size.

The Weaving Fork

The weaving fork, used to beat the weft into position, is another essential tool. Forks can be made of a hardwood branch or from a broken hammer or ax handle. You can buy weaving forks (see Sources of Supply) or make your own.

How to make a weaving fork

You will need a piece of hard, heavy wood that measures about 1/2 by 2 by 12 inches (1.25 by 5 by 30 cm). Using the fork pattern above, draw the basic shape on the wood and contour it by rasping, filing, and sanding. The fork should be 1/2 inch (1.25 cm) thick in the middle and slightly thinner at the edges.

Make the fork tines by sawing straight lines about 2 inches (5 cm) long and spaced about 1/4 inch (6 mm) apart. Taper the tines by carving and sanding the wood. The space between the tines should be wide enough so as not to bind the warp threads while beating.

Other Tools

You need to gather a few more tools. A curved 5-inch (13-cm) sacking needle is used at the end of the weaving when it is difficult to insert the weft. Sacking needles are sharp and can split warps, so dull the point by scraping it against a rock or sandpaper.

Another tool used at the end of the weaving is a round (ungrooved) umbrella rib, which can be used like a long needle. Old umbrellas and some children's umbrellas have the right kind of ribs. If the eye in the rib isn't big enough to

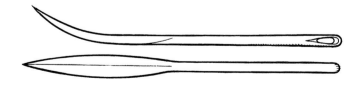

Sacking needle, top and side views.

thread the yarn through, make a loop of string to use as an eye, as shown in the drawing.

The umbrella rib, although of great help in the weaving, is not indispensable. You can use a very small (1/4-inch [6-mm]) batten instead.

Yarn

A Navajo rug is made up of three types of yarn. The warp, a thin, tightly spun yarn, is strung on the loom. It needs strength to withstand great tension and resist the abrasive action of the fork.

The weft, a thicker, fluffier yarn, is woven between the strands of warp so as to completely cover them with a tapestry weave. The weft give Navajo rugs their beautiful texture.

The edging cord, a two-ply handspun yarn, is used on the ends and sides of the rug to increase durability.

Whether you spin the yarns yourself or purchase them, you need to know how to evaluate them to be sure you have the best yarns for your weaving.

Warp

If you are not a spinner, choose a commercial warp yarn that is strong, fine, tightly spun, and preferably four-ply, such as "Navajo Warp" available through Davidson Old Mill Yarn (see Sources of Information and Supplies). This multi-ply warp is extremely strong and abrasion-resistant, but it can be slippery. You'll need to use a bowline knot (see page 69) at the beginning and end as well as for repairs.

If you are a spinner, spin a very tight, thin warp yarn, then test the yarn.

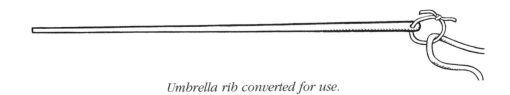

Umbrella rib converted for use.

Small finishing fork.

My mother always used to watch me weave. And when I didn't need the fork I would put it down and then pick it up again when I needed it. And my mother would say, "You just have to keep it in your hand all the time. When you get married, your mother-in-law will see you put it down and she will say, 'Let's just chase this girl away from here, she doesn't even know how to weave.'"

And even after she told me that, for a long time I still would lay it down, and my mother would always remind me. And sometimes I would just tell her, "It just slipped from my hand," or "I just put it down because I'm going to stop weaving for a while."

—Tiana Bighorse, Tuba City

Testing a warp yarn

Strength: Wrap the ends of a 2-foot (60-cm) sample of yarn around your hands, then pull hard. The yarn should not break or permanently stretch. Remember, the warp is the lifeline of your weaving and must withstand the tension of the loom.

Resilience and locking fibers: Good warp has some "give" to it, so wool warp yarns are well suited to the Navajo loom. Linen and cotton yarns are rigid and don't have the microscopic barbs that lock warp and weft together.

Abrasion resistance: Try abrading the yarn by rubbing your thumbnail back and forth along it multiple times to see how it will hold up to the repeated action of the fork. Good warp yarns resist abrasion. Warps that break or stretch when abraded require constant repair—an unnecessary frustration for the beginner.

Knot-holding ability: Good warp yarn must hold a knot. To test your warp, tie a square knot and then try to slide it between your index finger and thumbnail. Does the knot slip? If so, you should use a bowline (see page 69) instead of a square knot when warping the loom. Or you can secure the square knot by adding a drop of glue.

If your intended warp yarn does not pass these tests, spin it again and retest it—or buy another. Don't even think about warping your loom until you have a warp you trust.

Weft

The Sources of Information and Supplies on page 151 lists sources from which you can buy weft yarns that you can confidently use on your Navajo loom. Here are a few guidelines to consider when selecting weft yarns.

Navajo and other handspun

The fleece of today's Navajo sheep is fine and short-fibered. The yarn is spun on the Navajo spindle. Soft, fluffy, almost felted, it has surprising elasticity and strength.

Whether you buy handspun weft yarn or spin it yourself, you must not only consider the alluring color relationships of the yarns, but their uniformity of size and twist. Using large and small yarns, tightly and loosely spun yarns, or even just unevenly spun yarns in the same row will cause your weaving line to be uneven. Stripes will wiggle across the rug. Avoid irregular weft yarns on your first rug; constantly needing to fill in is a frustration for a beginning weaver.

APPROXIMATE WARP AND WEFT QUANTITIES		
Size of Project (length × width)	Minimum Warp Needed	Minimum Weft Needed
225 square inches (1452 cm)	50 yards (46 m)	1/2 lb. (22 kg)
450 square inches (2903 cm)	100 yards (91 m)	1 lb. (45 kg)
675 square inches (4355 cm)	150 yards (137 m)	1 1/2 lb. (68 kg)
900 square inches (5806 cm)	200 yards (183 m)	2 lb (91 kg)
1125 square inches (7258 cm)	250 yards (229 m)	2 1/2 lb. (113 kg)
1350 square inches (8710 cm)	300 yards (274 m)	3 lb. (136 kg)
1575 square inches (10,161 cm)	350 yards (320 m)	3 1/2 lb. (158 kg)
1800 square inches (11,613 cm)	400 yards (366 m)	4 lb. (181 kg)

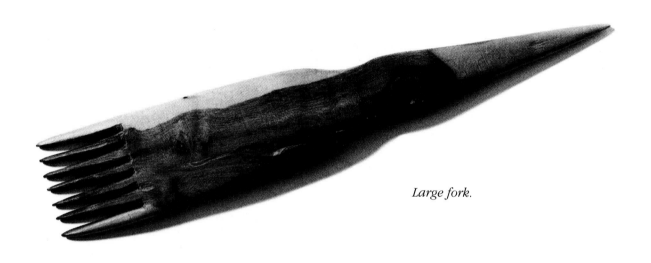

Large fork.

Sometimes after you have been weaving for a long time, the fork gets slippery from your body oils and slips from your hands. Then it always hits the floor right on its point. Sometimes it cracks. Whenever it gets slippery, you just have to wrap some yarn around the handle, or some tape, and that will fix it.

—Tiana Bighorse, Tuba City

Batten in warp.

Commercial single-ply yarns

You can buy commercial or mill-spun single-ply yarns in a varied range of colors. You can also purchase natural white, grey, and black, and overdye them. Commercial yarns have the advantage of being uniformly spun, but several brands, although they look good, can cause continual difficulty:

Avoid CUM, Mattgarn, which is overspun for Navajo weaving. Its cowhair content makes a scratchy final weave.

Australian yarns and others such as Icelandic Lopi are underspun. They must be respun before use. Used "as is," they overpack and break. Their softly spun long fibers make fuzzy design edges.

Plied yarns

Plied yarns are not used for Navajo weft. They have little elasticity, so they cause the edges of the weaving to pull in. They cannot be broken easily into wisps, and cut ends continually work their way to the surface of the weaving. Although you may be able to ravel, untwist, and break each end of a plied weft while weaving, the process is time-consuming and frustrating. Simply avoid it.

Warp/Weft Quantities and Warp Spacing

To determine how much warp and weft you need for your project, consult the chart on page 55.

The size of your weft yarns will determine the spacing of your warp.

When you use a weft yarn with about 200 yards (183 m) per 4-ounce (113-g) skein, space the warps 8 to the inch (2.5 cm), or space each warp turn 1/4 inch (6 mm) apart.

When you use a weft yarn with approximately 100 yards (91 m) per 4-ounce (113-g) skein, space warps 6 to the inch (2.5 cm), or space each warp turn 1/3 inch (8 mm) apart.

As you become a more proficient weaver, you may wish to experiment with finer weft yarns and closer warp spacing.

Edging Cord

The edging cord is a two-ply yarn that you make from the weft yarn.

To make edging cords for the top and bottom ends of your weaving, cut two lengths of weft yarn, each measuring four times the weaving width plus 50 inches (127 cm). For example, for a sampler 10 inches (25 cm) wide, cut two pieces of weft each 90 inches (228 cm) long.

Double each length back on itself. Twist it very tightly with a spindle, or between your hands, in the direction opposite to the initial spin. Hold the ends securely so the yarn can't untwist. Submerge the yarn in water until it is thoroughly wet. Tightly stretch the overspun yarn (between two trees, around the back of a chair, around a clothesline). Secure the ends. When the yarn is dry, the twist is set. The yarn may then be rolled into a ball and set aside until you are ready to use it.

To make edging cords for the sides or selvages of your weaving, cut two lengths of weft, each measuring four times the length of the weaving plus 20 inches (51 cm), and proceed to set the twist as described above.

Wide and narrow battens.

They say that if you break one of these things [batten or heddle rod] you'll get a sore back or sore arm. You just have to take care of them and put them in a safe place and not let the children play with them. I always tell them, "Put those down! Do you want Mommy to get sick?" And they just leave them alone. They know.

—Navajo weaver, Tuba City

---

4 The Navajo Loom

Don't pass anything through the loom. That's what they say. If someone is sitting on the other side and they want something, you can't hand it to them at the edge [of the rug] or through the warp. You just have to get up and take it around to them.

—Navajo weaver, Tuba City

A Navajo loom must be sturdy. Once mounted, warp will be tightly tensioned, and loom must bear the stress. Uprights can be two trees growing the right distance apart. Two poles of the hogan. Even a bedframe. Anything square and sturdy. Use what you have on hand that works. Adapt to the resources about you. Cut crosspieces of straight, strong limbs. Attach them with baling wire. Good. Use broom handles to hold the warp. And willows growing along the wash for shed sticks.

Making a loom is a project in itself. It tests your knowledge of your environment. Your resourcefulness. Your willingness to give each situation the energy required. Your determination to lay a good foundation.

Be patient. Soon you will sit at the loom's base on a pile of soft sheepskins. The tapestry of bright colors and intricate patterns will rise before you. . . .

Constructing a Small Loom

If you are just beginning to weave, start with a loom about 3 by 4 feet (91 by 122 cm), as shown on page 62. This loom is easy to construct and fits in the trunk of an average-sized car, so it is easy to transport. Later, you may want to build a larger, stationary loom.

Loom design

The loom should be larger than the weaving. Allow at least 1 foot (30 cm) of clearance at the top and 6 inches (15 cm) on each side.

A weaver needs free access to the width of the loom. Design your loom so that the uprights (the vertical posts) are supported by a flat horizontal base—not braced from the front.

The weaving needs to be held in front of the uprights so that they do not interfere when you insert the batten. Make your top and bottom

It's okay to pass things through the loom as long as the top beam isn't on it. Then it's not really a loom.

—Tiana Bighorse, Tuba City

beams longer than the width of the loom to hold the warp forward.

Build the loom so that it is solid, with no extraneous side motion. Use steel corner braces on the rear of the loom frame. Build the loom so that it is heavy to counter the pull of shed rods. For a loom 3 by 4 feet (91 by 122 cm), add a flat crosspiece in front on which the weaver can lean while stabilizing the loom. A back crosspiece also provides stability, especially if ballasted with rocks, cinder blocks, or other weights. Crosspieces are not always necessary on larger, heavier looms.

Supplies and tools

Be sure to select straight two-by-fours (about 4 × 9 cm) and dowels:

- 4 two-by-fours (about 4 × 9 cm), 34 inches (86 cm) long: for crosspieces
- 2 two-by-fours (about 4 × 9 cm), 42 inches (107 cm) long: for vertical posts, or uprights
- 2 two-by-fours (about 4 × 9 cm), 30 inches (76 cm) long: for legs
- 2 1-inch (2.5-cm) dowels or 3/4-inch (2.5-cm) metal pipes, 36 inches (91 cm) long: for beams

- 4 flat corner brackets, $3\frac{1}{2}$ × 5/8 inches (9 × 1.5 cm)
- 16 flathead wood screws, #6 (about 3 mm diameter) × 3/4 inches (2 cm)
- 4 machine bolts, 5/16 (8 mm) × $3\frac{1}{2}$ inches (9 cm)
- 4 nuts, 5/16 inches (8 mm)
- 8 flat washers
- 1/4 pound (113 g) 10-penny (about 7.5 cm long and 4 mm diameter) box nails
- 4 two-hole pipe straps, for 3/4-inch (2.5-cm) pipe (substitutions: bailing wire, leather bootlaces, etc.)
- 4 flathead wood screws, #6 (about 3mm diameter) × 3/4 inches (2 cm)
- Hammer, adjustable wrench, pliers, screwdriver, drill and 5/16-inch (8-mm) drill bit, rough sandpaper

Construction procedure

As you assemble the loom, refer to the drawing on page 62 to see how the parts fit together.

1. Nail two of the 34-inch (86-cm) crosspieces to two of the 42-inch (107-cm) uprights so that the frame dimensions are 34 by 45 inches (86 by 114 cm).

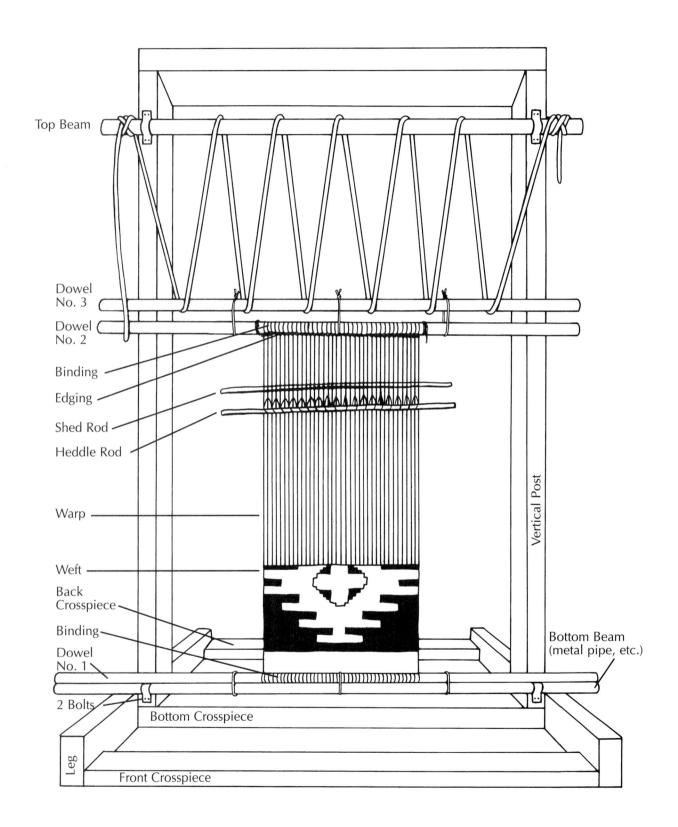

Top Beam

Dowel
No. 3

Dowel
No. 2

Binding

Edging

Shed Rod

Heddle Rod

Warp

Weft

Back
Crosspiece

Binding

Dowel
No. 1

2 Bolts

Bottom Crosspiece

Leg

Front Crosspiece

Vertical Post

Bottom Beam
(metal pipe, etc.)

62

I never asked my grandmother why not, but she always told me not to. She also said, "Don't let the children walk through the frame. Always place it against the wall." If the child is just small and not yet talking, then they say he will never try and will just be deaf and dumb. That's what she said.

—Navajo weaver, Tuba City

2. Screw in the four flat corner brackets to brace the rear of the frame.

3. Nail the two 30-inch (76-cm) legs to the remaining crosspieces to make the base of the loom.

4. Set the frame upright inside the base, centered between the front and rear crosspieces. Drill two 5/16-inch (8-mm) holes through the leg and upright on each side of the loom. Slide a washer onto a bolt, and insert it through one of the holes; add a second washer, then a nut, and tighten the bolt partway. Insert bolts into the other three holes the same way. Finish tightening all the bolts with the wrench and pliers.

5. Attach the top beam close to the top crosspiece. If you are using pipe straps, screw them onto the front of the uprights. If you are using bailing wire or leather bootlaces, drill holes through the uprights and thread the wire or leather through the holes and around the top beam several times.

6. Attach the bottom beam to the base of the upright by screwing pipe straps into position. Be sure the bottom beam rests on the legs of the frame.

7. Use sandpaper to smooth the rough places in the wood.

Working with Large Looms

To make a loom suitable for weaving rugs 3 by 5 feet (91 by 152 cm) or larger, follow the same procedure as when building a small loom, but consider the following:

You will need larger timbers to make the loom

Helen Nesbah Tsinnie, in front of her loom, with a Storm Pattern rug in progress.

sturdy. Consider two-by-six (about 4×14 cm), two-by-eight (about 4×19 cm), or even two-by-twelve (about 4×29 cm) uprights.

Log looms, although more difficult to build, are a lovely, natural-looking alternative to lumber-built looms.

Tightening the warp on a large loom requires great effort. When Tiana Bighorse's mother wove large rugs on a loom with uprights the size of telephone poles, her husband hitched up his team of horses to provide the necessary tightening power. Today some weavers connect the warp to the top beam with turnbuckles. By turning all buckles evenly, it's easy then to tighten the warp.

A large loom can function as a room divider, but make sure to position it so that natural light does not shine in the weaver's eyes. If necessary, hang a dark cloth behind the warp while you are weaving to block the light.

5 Warping the Loom

Face east when you are warping the loom. . . . When you are doing the edging cord, start with the east and circle the warp the same as the direction of the sun—east, south, west, north. Use some warp of a different color, like grey or darker, in one place. It represents rain.

—Navajo weaver, The Gap

When shall you warp your loom? Not when the hogan is filled with relatives and friends. Not in spare moments between herding your flock and setting rounds of fry bread into hot oil. No. You wait for solitude. For a time when the children will be gone. And no one will bump your loom! Be patient.

In time, warping begins. You wind with exacting tension. Twine edges to space warps and finish the ends. Bind warp to pipes, transfer to loom and lash, tension with rope. Your weaving will be straight and square. A job well done!

Don't count blisters. As some Navajo women say, "Think forward."

Think Forward

Warping the loom is the foundation of weaving. The catalyst for design. It sets weaving in motion, ideas flowing. Some Navajo weavers say: Never plan the design until you start to warp the loom. A warped loom is almost impossible to resist.

Other weavers say: As soon as you finish one weaving, start preparations for the next. The loom must be rewarped within four days: a day for the East, a day for the South, a day for the West, a day for the North.

But as exhilarating as it is to warp and to begin interacting with the design in your mind, precision must temper the process. It is better to avoid making mistakes than to have to correct them later. For sometimes they are never made right.

Weavers who spiritually care about weaving have certain taboos concerning warping. For instance, once begun, warping cannot be interrupted by eating, drinking, spitting, or sleeping. Process receives full attention.

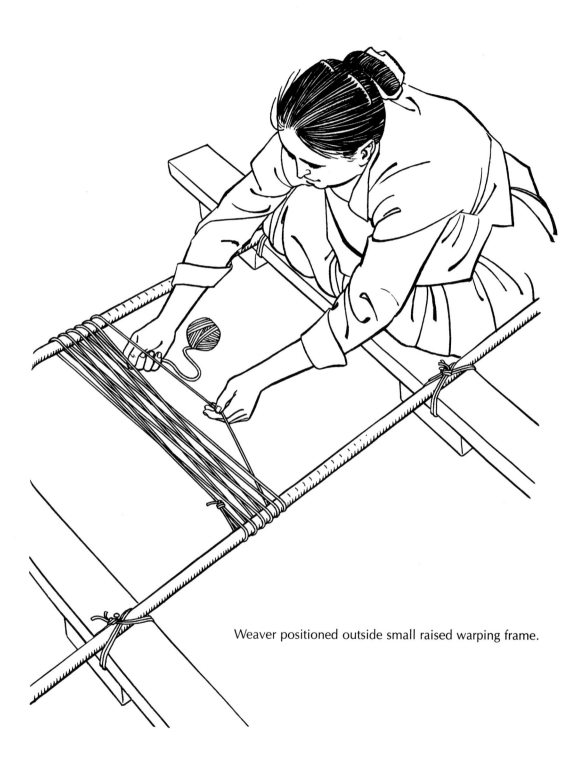

Weaver positioned outside small raised warping frame.

Step-by-Step Warping Directions

These are the directions for making the warp for the 10- by 23-inch (25- by 58-cm) sampler described in Chapter Seven. General comments that apply to making warps of other sizes are indicated with asterisks.

Step 1: Make a temporary warping frame

Materials and tools

Be sure to select straight two-by-fours (about 4 × 9 cm) and dowels.

- 2 two-by-fours (about 4 × 9 cm), at least 3 feet (91 cm) long: They should exceed the width of the weaving by at least 1 foot (30 cm) and are reusable.
- 2 1-inch (2.5-cm) dowels or broomsticks, wider than the loom
- 4 big nails
- hammer
- ball of heavy twine

Procedure

Refer to the drawing on page 67.

1. Place the two-by-fours (about 4 × 9 cm) on the floor about 30 inches (76 cm) apart. (The distance should be greater than the width of the weaving.)

2. Hammer two nails in each two-by-four (about 4 × 9 cm), 20½ inches (52 cm) apart. Leave the nailheads sticking out 1 inch (2.5 cm). (*The distance between the nails should be 2½ inches [6 cm] less than the desired length of the completed weaving.)

3. Lay the dowels across the two-by-fours (about 4 × 9 cm), to the outside of the nails. Tie the dowels in place with twine. Make sure the frame is square.

4. Raise the frame off the floor by setting the corners on four equal-sized objects (bricks, blocks of wood, books, or rocks, for example). Raise the frame high enough so that you can roll a ball of warp yarn underneath it.

5. Do not proceed unless you have two uninterrupted hours ahead of you. (A skilled weaver may require only one hour.)

Step 2: Wind the warp on the temporary frame

Materials and tools

- ball of warp, at least 53 yards (48 m). (*See page 55 to determine the amount of yardage needed for weavings of other dimensions.)
- scissors
- ruler
- pencil
- masking tape

Procedure

1. To warp the small sampler, sit outside the frame (see page 67). Be careful not to bump it. (*When warping large rugs, Navajo weavers sit inside the frame.)

2. A Navajo warp is one continuous strand wound in a figure eight around the two dowels of the temporary frame. Although Navajo weavers space their warp by eye, beginning weavers should mark lines in the center of both dowels at 1/4-inch (6-mm) intervals. These intervals will result in spacing of 8 warps per inch (2.5 cm). (*Weft for a larger rug may require a different warp spacing.) Label the dowel on your left No. 1. Number the dowel on your right No. 2. Mark 41 lines along 10 inches (25 cm) at the center of dowel No. 1. Mark 40 lines along 9¾ inches (24.75 cm) at the center of dowel No. 2.

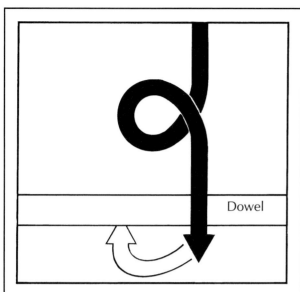

Preliminary looping of the bowline knot.

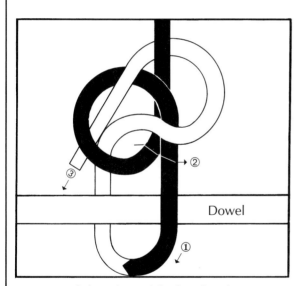

Final threading of the bowline knot.

Tightening the knot under tension

Pull down on strand #1 going over the dowel.

Hold the tightened loop between the thumb and forefinger of your left hand. Pull up on strand #2 above the loop until you have achieved the right amount of tension.

Pull down on the end of strand #3 to anchor the knot and maintain the tension.

3. Tie the end of the warp yarn to dowel No. 1, positioning the loop on the mark farthest from you. Traditional weavers use the square knot, but we recommend the bowline or weaver's knot, which will not slip. The knot should be 2 inches (5 cm) away from the dowel.

4. Hold the warp yarn tied to dowel No. 1 in your left hand and the ball of warp in your right hand. Place the ball over dowel No. 2 and then roll it back toward the middle of the frame. Continue to hold the warp yarn in your left hand with constant tension.

5. With your right hand, grasp the yarn coming off of the ball, pull it until the slack is taken up, freeing your left hand, and hold the yarn securely. The tension should be snug but not binding. Notice how much tension you are applying and maintain this tension throughout the warping procedure. Consistent tension is critical!

6. Continue to hold the yarn in your right hand with constant tension. Pick up the ball with your left hand, place it over dowel No. 1, and roll it back toward the middle of the frame. With your left hand, pick up the yarn coming off of the ball and pull it until the slack is taken up, freeing your right hand.

7. With your right hand, adjust the loops so that they are each on a mark, 1/4 inch (6 mm) apart. Continue warping. Follow the rhythm: Over and around under. Hold. Over and around under. Hold. Establishing a rhythm helps to keep the tension constant.

Continue to position warp on alternate dowels at 1/4-inch (6-mm) intervals. Each time a warp is carried over the dowel and returned back under to the center of the frame, it is referred to as a warp turn. At four

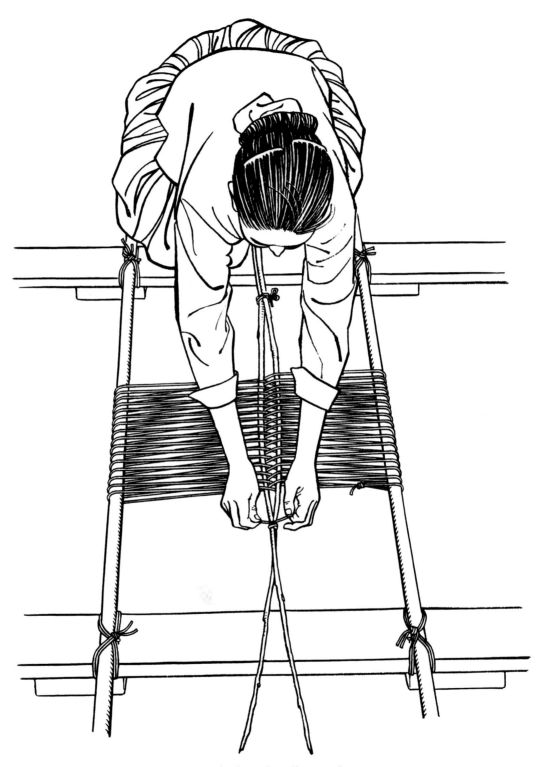

Preserving sheds with willow sticks.

Always finish it [the warping] at one time, because if you stop when you have just about that much [seven inches] to go and you still have a ball of warp, then when you start again it never is the same as before. And then the rug just goes like this [indicating longer on one side than the other]. The same thing happens if someone bumps it, or the children are running around. They always say you have to keep the children out.

—Navajo weaver, Cameron

turns per inch (2.5 cm) there should be 40 turns on dowel No. 2; counting the crosses in the center of the frame, there should be 80 individual warps.

The last warp turn will encircle dowel No. 1. Hold this last turn in place on the outside of the dowel with a piece of masking tape to secure the tension.

8. Tie the end of the warp to dowel No. 1, using a bowline knot tied under tension (see page 69). The knot should be 2 inches (5 cm) away from the dowel. You may have to practice the bowline knot several times—off and on the loom—before you get it right. Cut off the excess warp, 1 inch (2.5 cm) away from the knot. Trim excess yarn from the first knot, too.

Step 3: Preserve the sheds

Materials

- 2 willow sticks, about 10 inches (25 cm) longer than the width of the weaving (substitution: 3/4-inch [2-cm] dowels)
- ball of twine

Procedure

Refer to the drawing on page 70.

The figure eight established during the warping process is the first step in creating the two sheds you need in weaving. Preserve the cross in the warp as follows:

1. Place a shed rod in each loop of the figure eight. Simply slide a shed rod alongside dowel No. 2 and through the warp turns.

71

Ball of warp.

Sitting with the length of dowel No. 1 in front of you, insert the shed rod from right to left, under the knot you tied last, through the warp turns, and over the knot you tied first.

2. Slide the two shed rods gently toward the center of the frame. The cross will be between them.

3. Tie the ends of the shed rods snugly together with twine.

Step 4:
Space the warp turns with edging cord

Materials

• 2 edging cords, made according to directions on page 58. Make them well in advance of warping, so they will be dry when needed. For the sampler, the cords should be about 45 inches (114 cm) long.

Procedure

Refer to drawings below and on page 74.

To space the warps and form a permanent edging, Navajo weavers twine the warp turns together with a heavy two-ply edging cord. The color of the edging cord usually matches the first and last colors woven, but it can be a contrasting color.

1. Kneel or sit with the length of dowel No. 1 in front of you. Double one length of the edging cord. Tie an overhand knot in the folded end, forming a 5-inch (13-cm) loop. Slip one end of the cord through the first turn of the warp on the left end of the dowel. With your right hand, pull the cord through until the loop knot is next to the warp turn. You now have one strand of the cord within the first warp turn and one strand outside of it.

2. Hold the strand within the warp in your

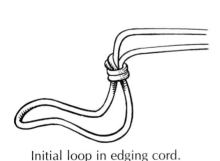

Initial loop in edging cord.

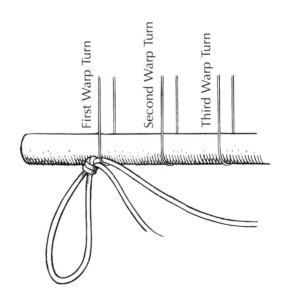

First Warp Turn

Second Warp Turn

Third Warp Turn

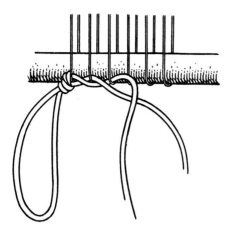

Twining edging cord.

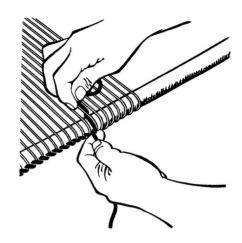

Hand position for twining.

right hand and the free strand in your left. Cross the right strand over the left. Hold this cross with your left hand—index finger under, thumb on top—and don't let go. You now have a twist in the edging cord between the first and second warp turns. The twisted cord holds the warp turns the proper distance apart. (*For a fine weave, one twist is enough. In heavier weaves, two or even three twists of the edging cord are needed to space the warps farther apart.)

3. With your right hand, slip the bottom cord under the second warp turn and cross it over the other strand. Secure the cross with your left hand as before. The second warp turn is now stabilized.

4. Continue twisting strands of the cord between the warp turns. The rhythm is: Under the warp and over the cord. Hold. Under the warp and over the cord. Hold. Each warp turn should stay on the mark. Be sensitive to how tightly you are twisting; beginners tend to twist too tightly, which results in warps that are too close together and off their marks.

When you reach the right edge of the dowel, tie the ends of the strands together snugly with an overhand knot. Measure the warp width to be certain that it is 10 inches (25 cm) wide (*or your intended width). Cut off any excess edging cord, 5 inches (13 cm) beyond the knot.

5. Repeat the same procedure along dowel No. 2. When you have finished, measure again to insure that the warp is the correct width. If one side is too wide or too narrow, simply slide the warp turns closer together or father apart as needed, and retie the knot.

6. Closely examine both sides of the warp to be certain each individual warp turn is bound.

This part of warping is complete, and you can now stop to eat or sleep. Or if you wish, continue to the next step: binding the edged warp so that it is ready to be mounted on the loom.

Step 4: Bind the edged warp to two dowels

Materials

• 1 1-inch (2.5-cm) dowel, 36 inches (91 cm)

long: Number this dowel No. 1 and, as before, center 41 marks at 1/4-inch (6-mm) intervals along 10 inches (25 cm).

- ball of strong twine: Cut two 160-inch (4-m) lengths. Any strong twine is sufficient, but we recommend Puritan™ Wrapping Twine (Wellington Leisure Products, Inc., Madison, GA 30650). Navajo weavers prefer a strong two-ply handspun yarn that can withstand the tension of the loom.

Procedure

Position yourself with the length of the old dowel No. 1 in front of you.

1. Lay the new dowel No. 1 along the old dowel No. 1 outside the frame. Cut the left loop of the edging cord and tie the two ends very tightly around the new dowel, to the left of the new markings. Untie the overhand knot on the right side of the old dowel and retie the ends of the edging cord to the right of the markings on the new dowel.

   When the edging cord is secured to the new dowel at both ends, remove the old dowel No. 1 by carefully sliding it out of the warp turns. Erase one outside mark on this dowel, relabel it as new dowel No. 2, and set it aside for later use.

2. Roll the twine into a tight ball. Tightly wrap the edging cord tied to the left side of the new dowel three times with the twine. Wrap the twine over the dowel and away from you. Pull the twine so it is very tight. Make sure the ends of the edging cord are well secured.

3. Continue wrapping the twine once around the dowel between each warp turn. Keep the warp turns aligned with the marks on the dowel; the turns of the wrapped twine should fall between them. Pull the twine very tight! Brace the dowel to keep it from rotating.

   If you have trouble discerning which warp strands constitute a warp turn, brace the warping frame and pull the dowel closer to you to put the yarns under tension.

4. When you reach the right side of the dowel, bind the ends of edging cord securely with

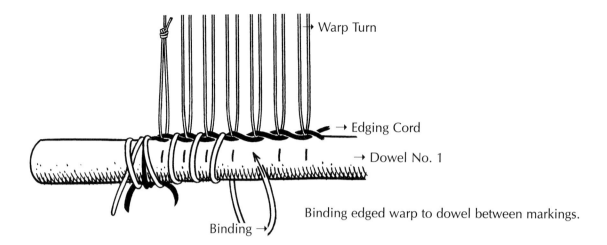

Warp Turn

→ Edging Cord

→ Dowel No. 1

Binding →

Binding edged warp to dowel between markings.

three wraps of twine, as you did on the left side. Tuck the end of the twine beneath the last two wraps before pulling it tight.

5. Repeat this procedure on old dowel No. 2, replacing it with the dowel you labeled new No. 2. Be certain to remeasure the width of the warp and adjust it if necessary.

6. The warp is now suspended between two dowels and bound to each by means of strong twine. Double-check your binding to be sure you have wrapped between the warp turns. Test any warp turns that look split by giving one of the warp strands in it a tiny tug. The warp strand that moves should be within the same binding wrap, not in the wrap next to it.

The next steps are very easy. You are in the homestretch.

Step 6:
Mount the warp on the upright loom

Materials

- old dowel No. 2, renumbered as dowel No. 3
- ball of heavy twine, 8 lengths each at least 20 inches (51 cm)
- extra 1-inch (2.5-cm) dowel or pipe: for spacer
- sacking needle
- 3/8-inch (9-mm) twisted cotton rope, 15 feet (4.5 m) long (substitute: doubled cotton clothesline; do not use hemp or nylon).

Procedure

Refer to the drawing on page 78.

1. Fasten dowel No. 3 to dowel No. 2 with three pieces of doubled twine. Tie one doubled piece at each end. With a sacking needle, thread the doubled twine between the dowel and the edging cord at the middle of the warp before tying it. Use the spacer to hold the dowels uniformly 1 inch (2.5 cm) apart.

2. Center the warp between the loom uprights. Fasten dowel No. 1 (the one on which the ends of the warp are knotted) to the bottom beam of the loom. As before, tie the dowel and beam together at the ends and in the middle, pulling dowel No. 1 flush against the beam and leaving no space between them.

Grace Homer, winding warp onto the frame.

When stringing up the loom, if you have to leave and you are only half finished, you have to take it all off and put it away and when you come back you have to do it all at one time.

—Navajo weaver, The Gap

3. Attach one end of the rope to the left side of the top beam, just outside the left edge of the loom. Bind dowel No. 3 to the top beam by encircling both of them from left to right in what Navajo women call the "sunwise" direction.

To do this, wind the rope over the top beam and bring it back underneath dowel No. 3. When you reach the right side, secure the rope by wrapping it around the top beam several times and tucking the end of the rope through its own wraps.

Step 7: Tighten the warp

Procedure

The warp should be tight and resistant, but not rigid. It should have a tension somewhat like

Rope position for mounting warp to upright loom.

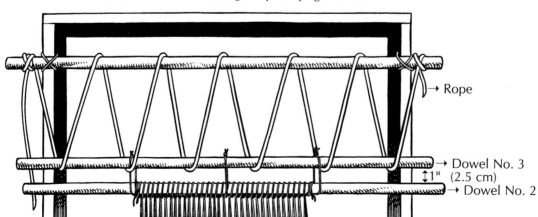

Rope

Dowel No. 3
↕1" (2.5 cm)
Dowel No. 2

Grace Homer, mounting warp to her loom.

Shed sticks must be strong and straight. Cut them green and dry them attached to broom stick to keep them straight. Willow is good, but you can use salt cedar [tamarisk] if you can't find willow.

—Tiana Bighorse, Tuba City

guitar strings. This tautness allows you to beat down the weft and weave it compactly. It also helps you keep your edges straight. To tighten the warp, cinch the rope from right to left:

1. With your left hand, pull down decisively on the section of rope that crosses in front of dowel No. 3 (the third wrap from the right in the drawing on page 78). While continuing to pull downward with your left hand, use your right hand to push repeatedly on the section of rope just to the right of and behind the section you are pulling. The combination of push-release, push-release on a back rope while maintaining a steady downward pull on a front rope results in a powerful cinching action. By pulling, the left hand forces the rope to take up the slack generated by pushing with the right.

2. Transfer the now tightened rope in your left hand to your right hand. Do not release the tension! Your left hand is now free to grasp the next left front section of rope and pull down tightly to take up the slack. As before, with your right hand, push-release several times on the section of rope to the right of

and behind the section you are pulling.

3. Continue cinching and tightening the rope, working from right to left across the full width of the loom. When you get to the left end, retie the rope to secure it.

4. Repeat the tightening procedure several times until the warp is very taut. You must tighten the warp periodically throughout the weaving process, but especially while weaving the first half of the rug. It is very important to maintain the correct amount of tension while weaving. If the side edges or selvages become uneven, or the rug begins to ripple, or the batten keeps turning flat instead of staying on edge, you need to tighten the warp.

Step 8: Position the shed rods

Materials

- medium-weight cotton string, at least 160 inches (4 m) for the sampler. String should be smooth, soft, and unpolished. (*Multiply number of warp turns by 4 inches [10 cm] to estimate how much you need for other size projects.)

Procedure

The two shed rods you used to preserve the cross in the warp are also needed for the weaving process. You use them to raise and lower alternate warp threads to create the two sheds through which the weft travels.

The upper shed rod is already in place; it is the topmost shed rod inserted to maintain the figure eight. This rod holds alternate warps in a forward position. With the lower shed rod, or heddle rod, the weaver pulls forward the warps that pass behind the upper shed rod.

Navajo weavers depend on the flexible willow for perfect shed rods. They pick straight branches, whittle off the nobs, and tie them to a broomstick to dry. The upper shed rod should have about the same diameter as a pencil; the heddle rod, slightly less. The flexibility of the willow allows the weaver to pull warp yarns forward in sections. (You can substitute tamarisk sticks, or as a last resort, 1/4-inch [6-mm] dowels. Be warned, dowels are rigid and slippery and tend to fall out of the loom.)

To prepare the heddle rod, follow these steps:

1. Untie the shed rods that preserve the figure eight in your warp. Slide the upper shed rod to the top of loom. Slide the lower rod to about 6 inches (15 cm) below the upper rod.

2. From right to left, insert a batten immediately below the lower rod. Turn the batten on edge. Be sure that the batten exactly replaces the rod in relation to the warps; then remove the rod.

3. Just above the batten, insert one end of the cotton string and pull it through from right to left. The end should extend 2 inches (5 cm) beyond the left side of the warp; the ball of string should be on the right side of the loom. Tie a 1-inch (2.5-cm) loop in the left end of the string using an overhand knot.

4. You are now ready to place heddle loops onto the heddle rod, working from left to right. With your left hand, hold the heddle rod horizontally level with the looped end of the string. Insert the right end of the heddle rod into the loop.

5. With your right index finger, reach between the first and second warps that cross the batten and pull the string out so as to create a 1½-inch (4-cm) loop. Give the loop a three-quarter turn to the right and place this loop onto the heddle rod next to the first. Pull the string from the right side of the loom to take up any slack.

6. Repeat the procedure to form heddle loops across the warp. Move the heddle rod to the right as you create each successive loop.

   Continue until all the warps crossing the batten are looped and attached to the heddle rod. When you reach the right side of the loom, tie the final loop in the heddle string with an overhand knot, as you did on the left side, and insert the rod. Cut off any extra string about 1/2 inch (1 cm) away from both knots.

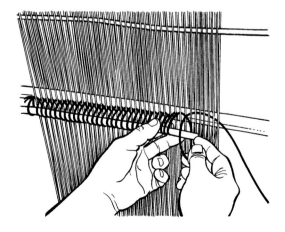

Looping heddles onto heddle rod.

81

Grace Homer, at her big loom.

If you're not going to weave for about three days, loosen nanoolzhee'

[the warp] a little. You don't have to do it all the time, not for just short

times away, only if it's a long time. That's just what I do.

—Navajo weaver, Cameron

You don't have to do it [warping] in any certain direction. Just do it wherever there is nothing [in the way].

—Navajo weaver, Tuba City

7. Pull the heddle rod forward to make sure that every warp that crosses the batten has been looped on the rod. If you have looped them all, you can now remove the batten. If you haven't, you need to remove the rod and rethread it through to pick up the skipped heddles.

Step 9: Check the tension of the warp

Check the warp. It should be absolutely vertical and uniformly taut from side to side. To feel the tension, press your fingers across the warp.

If one section is looser than the rest, retighten the warp. Working across the warp from the tight section toward the loose section, pull each consecutive front warp firmly and evenly to take up the slack. (If you are working from left to right, pull up on each front warp. If working from right to left, pull down on each forward warp.) Repeat the process as necessary until all the warp strands feel the same when you press your fingers against them. Then retie the end with a bowline knot under tension (see page 69).

Step 10: Side selvage cords

Most Navajo weavings have edging cords on the sides as well as on the ends. You do not need them for the sampler. See Chapter Eight for directions on how to install them on your other weavings.

The Basics of 6
Navajo Weaving

A traditional weaver also believes that when you're finishing a rug, you should sing your weaving song to make your weaving ending easier. But today not very many weavers know the song.

—Navajo weaver, Gallup

The loom stands ready. Tools and yarns await. It is wise to focus your thoughts ahead. To look back would be to remember the countless hours of preparation and effort already spent. And the design itself is not yet begun.

So you review possible patterns: There are those Mother makes; there are those Grandmother used to make. You hold them in your mind. Expectations mount; for color and design to enfold you; beauty to hold you. But first, you must become One with the tools. A part of the loom. This is the Weaving Way.

Counting Design

Navajo weavers count the pattern by inserting the batten and counting the warp pairs that cross it. When a Navajo weaver says, "This [design] should be two warps here," she means two pairs of warps, or four warp threads. This way, each element of the design contains an even number of warp threads. Even if a weaver says, "Three warps here," she is referring to three pair—six individual strands. Counting only the forward warp pairs—half of the total number—makes it easier to count the design.

How to Mark the Center

Most Navajo rug designs are vertically and horizontally symmetrical, so you need to mark the center of the warp in both directions.

Marking the horizontal center

Count the warp pairs from each side to find the center of the warp. Tie a string around the two center warps and then push the string to the top of the weaving, out of the way. A marked center gives you an immediate reference point, which makes it easier to count the pattern throughout the weaving process.

Marking the vertical center

A Navajo weaver may mark the vertical center by first measuring the height of the warp with a string. She folds the string in half, and uses this to gauge the vertical center of the rug. She then marks a dark line across the center four warps.

If each half of the weaving will contain a complete design, she folds the doubled string in half again to mark the quarter and three-quarter points. These marks help the weaver gauge the symmetry of the design while weaving.

If you prefer greater accuracy, you can use a measuring tape.

Making the Sheds

The basic weave structure in Navajo technique is the tapestry weave. Weft completely covers the warp threads in two alternating rows:

Row 1. Over, under, over, under . . .
Row 2. Under, over, under, over . . .

The sheds are the openings between the front and back warps that make the tapestry weave possible. The two alternating sheds are made with the shed rods. The rods hold alternate warps forward so that the weaver can insert the weft between them.

The stick-shed is made with the rods positioned close together. The pull-shed is made with the rods apart.

Holding the batten, strumming the warp

With your right hand, hold the batten at its center from underneath as shown in the drawing. The curved end of the tool should be to your left, with the longer, boat-shaped edge up. Rest the bottom edge of the batten on the base of your index finger and on the tip of your third finger. Hold the top of the batten between the tips of your index finger and thumb. Hold the tool comfortably; it should feel centered and balanced.

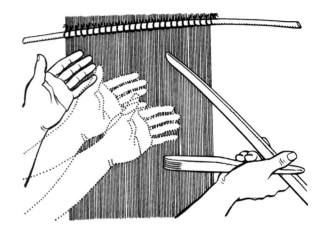

Position of batten, ready for insertion. Strumming technique to separate warps. (Note position of fork when not in use.)

The fibers of a wool warp stick together. To separate them, strum the warp threads from right to left with your left hand, using the backs of your fingers. This is a standard hand movement, which you should repeat before inserting the batten in the pull-shed. At the beginning of a weaving, you may need to strum before inserting your batten in both sheds. Later, as the loose fibers wear off the warp, you may only need to strum before using the pull-shed.

Here's how to work the two sheds. Practice the process several times before you begin to weave so that you will be comfortable with the workings of the loom.

Making the stick-shed

With your left hand, position the shed rods together so that the upper rod lies on the heddle loops at about eye level. With your right hand, insert the batten from right to left, curved end first, into the opening just below both rods. When the batten is through and centered on the warp, reach up with your left hand and push both rods up out of the way. Then grasp the ends of the batten with both hands and turn it on edge so that the top edge faces you (see page 103). (Because of the shape it forms, in legend the batten is the rainbow.)

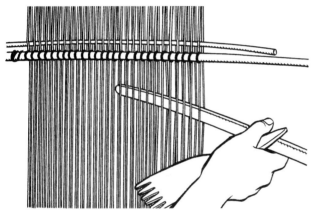

Position of shed and heddle rods to create stick shed.

When inserting the batten, make sure you do not pick up any of the wrong warp strands. When weaving, you will insert weft in the clear passageway below the batten.

Return the batten to a flat position. To remove it, pull the batten halfway out of the warp with your right hand; then grasp it from underneath at its center and continue pulling. The batten is now in the correct position in your hand to be inserted into the next shed. Keep the batten in your hand while changing sheds. If you put it down, you have to relocate it, pick it up again, and reposition it in your hand. Much time will be lost, and the weaving rhythm broken. It is the mark of a skilled weaver to retain the weaving tools in hand when they are not in use.

Making the pull-shed

With your left hand, push up both shed sticks and strum the warps. Then pull down the heddle rod about 6 inches (15 cm) below the upper shed rod—about eye level. Grasp the heddle rod near its right end and pull it firmly so that the back warps come forward. Insert the batten as far as it will comfortably go just behind the heddles.

Release your left hand, grasp the heddle rod further to the left, pull forward again, and continue to insert the batten. Repeat this process

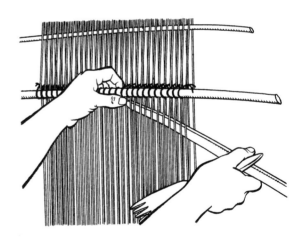

Position of shed and heddle rods to create pull shed.

across the loom until the batten has been inserted all the way through. Remove the batten from the pull-shed as you did from the stick-shed.

The root of it all is The Weaver's Song. If you know that then you can just do any kind of weaving, all designs.

—Navajo weaver, The Gap

The number of times you will need to grasp, pull, and release the heddle rod depends on several factors: the width of your rug, how well you separated your warps by strumming, how far you are in the weaving (toward the end it becomes harder to pull the heddles forward), the flexibility of your heddle rod, and the curve of your batten.

If the end of the batten keeps going behind the back warps instead of through the open shed, the batten may not be curved enough. Re-shape the batten as described on page 48 or replace the tool with a better one. A good curve is essential to pleasureable weaving.

Inserting Weft, Packing It Down

As it is being woven, the weft travels back and forth: from right to left in the stick-shed and from left to right in the pull-shed. Here are the basic techniques for inserting weft that you'll need to know to start. Read through them before you begin working on the sampler presented in Chapter Seven, and refer back to them whenever you have a question or problem. (A more detailed description of the techniques needed to weave stripes and patterns is presented in Chapters Seven and Eight.)

Adding a new piece of weft

In Navajo weaving, the weft yarn is always broken, never cut. Breaking the end gives it a natural taper that will blend with the other yarn fibers in the weaving and lock the wispy end into place. When you run out of yarn and want to add a piece, as long as the end is tapered the joint will be imperceptible. The same is true when you want to add a new color at the start of a design.

To break a strand of yarn, grasp it firmly with your hands spaced about 4 inches (10 cm) apart. Completely untwist the section of yarn that is between your hands. Then, pull the yarn until it breaks.

How to lay in a yarn

When you lay in your first weft or the weft to start a new design, do not let the end hang out of the warp. Pull the yarn through the shed until the naturally tapered end is just inside the design area. You can also let the end extend beyond the design and simply finger-weave the wisp back into the design area in the opposite shed.

Don't be tempted to leave ends hanging out, intending to snip them later. These blunt ends will work their way to the surface of the weav-

Weaving in progress. This Navajo weaver sets up her warp differently and so she makes her hooked joints from right to left.

ing. A weaver who leaves yarn ends hanging out is considered neither a good weaver nor one who spiritually cares about the weaving process.

Piecing yarn within a design

When you run out of yarn within a stripe or design, do not use a knot to connect the new yarn with the old. Instead, overlap the wispy ends of the yarns about 1 inch (2.5 cm) and continue weaving in the same direction. The joint will be imperceptible.

Using a stick-shuttle

To make intricate designs on the Navajo loom, you will insert, hook, and piece colors together with your fingers. When you are making a simple design or stripe, it is much easier to insert the yarn with a stick-shuttle. Any straight stick with broken ends will do. The stick-shuttle should be longer than the width of the weaving.

To wind yarn onto the stick-shuttle, hold the broken yarn end between the index finger and thumb of your left hand. Twirl the rough broken end of the stick in the wispy yarn end to catch and hold the yarn. Tightly wrap the yarn around the end of the stick three times. Make five long wraps of yarn to encircle the stick to the opposite end. Now loop the yarn over that end of the stick and tightly wrap the yarn around the end three times.

Make five long wraps of yarn to return to the first end, and three more tight wraps at the end, just below the first wrappings. Repeat the process about four more times—to one end and back. Break the yarn about 20 inches (51 cm) from the end of the stick that you wrap last.

To use the stick-shuttle to weave a simple stripe, unwind enough yarn to cross the entire width of the weaving. Insert the shuttle through the shed just below the batten, and pack the yarn into place.

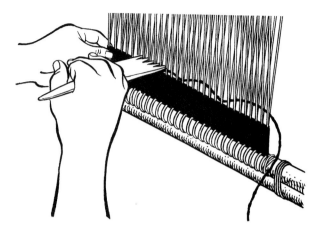

Scalloping weft to achieve correct tension. (Note position of fork when in use.)

Using the fork

Grasp the fork in your right hand, with your thumb underneath it and your fingers on top. With a flicking wrist motion, pushing down with your fingers, pack, or beat, the weft into position along the weaving line.

The most important thing to remember when using the fork is to retain it in your hand at all times. To hold it at rest and out of the way, use your fourth and fifth fingers to flick the tines downward against the heel of your hand (see drawing on page 86). This frees your first three fingers so that you can grasp the batten or manipulate the yarn.

You can also use the fork's pointed handle to separate warps that are too close together, as described on page 97.

Gauging vertical distances

When a stripe or design is as large as you want it to be, weave two or more rows before beginning the next color. The extra rows will compensate for the packing of the yarn that will occur when you beat down subsequent wefts.

You can tell if someone knows The Weaver's Song just by looking at their weaving.

—Tiana Bighorse, Tuba City

How to Regulate Weft Tension

Inconsistent and inappropriate weft tension causes most of the problems that occur in Navajo weaving. Navajo weavers regulate weft tension in two ways: they scallop the weft or they beat the weft on the bound edge.

When you are weaving in a striped area or a large design we suggest that you use the scallop. When you are creating more intricate designs, use the alternate method of beating the bound weft edge.

Making scallops

Draw the weft loosely through the shed. With your fingers or the point of the fork handle, press the weft almost to the weaving line at even intervals to form scallops. The size of the scallop will determine the amount of weft that will be packed in place with the fork.

As a rule of thumb, a weaving 10 inches (25 cm) wide requires four scallops—the peak of each should be about 3/4 inch (2 cm) from the weaving line. Another way to think about this is that it takes about 12 inches (30 cm) of weft to weave across a 10-inch (25-cm) warp. This rule cannot be used as an absolute measure,

however, as the size, spin, and elasticity of the yarn are also determining factors.

Scallops that are too high cause weft loops on the front and back surfaces of the fabric. Scallops that are too shallow cause the weaving to pull in. It is common for beginners to create scallops that are too shallow rather than too high. If you are uncertain whether or not you have the right tension, think loose. Remember, you want a tight warp and a relaxed weft.

To test your tension, scallop the yarn across one row and beat it down. Now pinch the yarn as it comes out of the shed and pull it taut. There should be about 2 inches (5 cm) of extra yarn between your pinched fingers and the edge of the weaving. If there is less than that, you should have made the scallops higher.

Beating the bound edge

Experienced weavers do not bother creating scallops. They have a feeling in their fingers for when and how much they should pull on the weft.

Beating the bound weft edge is like creating a continuous scallop ahead of the fork. With your left hand, hold the free end of the weft diagonally in the shed. If the yarn is traveling

Always sit up straight when you are weaving. My mother always told me that you should sit straight or you will spoil your straightness by weaving humped over at the loom. She says you would walk around hunched over with a hump on your back by the time you are thirty, unless you sit straight at the loom.

—Tiana Bighorse, Tuba City

from right to left, beat the weft with the fork from right to left, so that the bound end of the weft is hit first. When weaving left to right, hold the yarn diagonally in the shed with the left hand; cross the right hand under the left hand to beat the weft in place from left to right.

To master this technique, notice the amount of tension that your left hand applies to the weft, as well as the angle at which you are holding the yarn. Test the tension as you would when scalloping (see page 91).

Evaluating problems with weft tension

You are not allowing enough weft in the shed if:

- Warp is visible between the weft a few rows below the weaving line.

- The side selvages are pulling in.

- The warps are too close in some areas.

Remedy: Take out the weft that you have woven. As you reweave it, increase the height of the scallops.

You are allowing too much weft in the shed if:

- Loops are forming on the front or back surface of the fabric.

- The fabric is so elastic that when you pull on the edges, you can stretch it widthwise more than 1/2 inch (1.25 cm).

- The selvage edges are wider than the intended width of the project.

Remedy: Take out the weft that you have woven. As you reweave it, reduce the height of the scallops.

Working wtih the fork in hand.

"You can always tell those who spiritually care about their weaving— their loomspace is clear all around," Tiana Bighorse told me in 1970. The weaver and loom are one. What affects one, affects both.

Everything around gets woven into the rug. Wisps of yarn left lying about are caught and woven in. Loose hair from brushing floats about and is woven in. The weaver stops to remove them. The weaving rhythm is halted. The interruption is woven in.

Charles Loloma, Hopi silversmith, quotes his weaver-father: "It's not enough to weave beautiful rugs. You have to think beautiful thoughts while weaving them."

An angry weaver bangs hard, pulls yarns tight; sides go in. Thoughts, left lying about, get woven in.

But if you align yourself just as you do the loom—then in the clearness, you can hear the Song.

With beauty before me, it is woven
With beauty behind me, it is woven
With beauty above me, it is woven
With beauty below me, it is woven
And in beauty, it is finished.

—Halo of the Sun

Tiana Bighorse, packing warp with the fork.
At the top of her loom, a tied weft marks horizontal center.

Your tension is inconsistent if:

- The fabric is rippling.

Remedy: Remove the weft back to the point where the rippling begins. Reweave, correcting your tension.

Unraveling is not pleasant, but the amount of time that it takes you to unravel is insignificant compared to the amount of time you will spend living with your weaving, wishing you had taken the time to fix it.

Keeping the Edges Straight

Straight selvage edges are the sign of an accomplished weaver; uneven edges are the sign of a novice. Trying to make neat, straight edges can be exasperating for a beginning weaver. So we encourage you to measure the width of your weaving frequently. At the first sign of the slightest deviation, stop and correct the problem.

If the weaving is getting narrower

The most common difficulty in Navajo weaving is edges drawing in. It means the warp needs tightening and/or the weft needs to be laid in more loosely.

Often just before edges begin to pull in, the warps draw together about 1 inch (2.5 cm) or so just inside the selvage edge. As soon as you see that warps are beginning to get too close, remedy the problem immediately.

Remedies:

- Tighten the warp, if necessary.

- Watch the weft as it circles the edge of the weaving to be sure the warps at the edge are not being pulled in by the weft.

- Watch the color joints. The tension at the joint should be tight, but the weft that creates the design should be loose so that the row is relaxed.

- Tie the weaving snugly to the uprights about 1 inch (2.5 cm) below where you are weaving. The tension will help pull the edge out to its proper width. But unless you correct the cause of the problem, the edges will continue to pull in!

If the weaving is getting wider

The edges will widen if the warp is too loose, if the weft is laid in too loosely, or if the weft is too big for the spacing between the warps.

Remedies:

- Tighten the warp.

- Reduce the height of the scallops.

- Unspin the weft yarn and pull it to make it thinner. Respin it before beginning to weave again.

Keeping Warps Evenly Spaced

Keeping the warps evenly spaced is really, really, really important. You must maintain your awareness of the correct spacing throughout every phase of the weaving. During the warping process, the edging cord determines the initial warp spacing and the binding cord stabilizes it. During the weaving process, a tight warp maintains the spacing—as long as your weft tension is correct.

As you weave, constantly watch the warp spacing. If the warps start to draw together, you are laying the weft in too tightly or the weft is too thin to hold the warps apart. If you ignore the problem, it will get worse, and soon the edges will start to draw in. If you handle the problem immediately, it will quickly be resolved.

Navajo weavers redistribute warps as a matter of course—perhaps once every ten rows. Redistribute crowded warps as follows:

1. Remove a few rows of weft to ease the tension.

2. Working in the tight area, use the pointed handle of the fork to lift the last woven weft up as high as it will go. Then lift each successive weft underneath it until you have worked about 1 inch (2.5 cm) of the fabric. Working within the tight area, push left warps to the left, right warps to the right. Move warps with authority! The weft you lifted will hold the new warp spacing in place.

3. Hold the corrected warp spacing between the index finger and thumb of your left hand. With your right hand, slide the weft down into the center of the problem area. Beat the weft back in place with the fork, hitting the center of the trouble spot first to force the weft in and the warps out.

4. Continue weaving, making sure to put plenty of weft into this area to keep the warp spaces open.

Filling in Low Spots

You must keep the weaving line straight and level. As you weave, keep checking for low spots and correct and fill them immediately.

Most of the time, low spots are caused by warps that have moved too far apart in one area and have become too tight in the neighboring area. Warps spaced too far apart cause the weaving line to sag. Redistribute the warps that are too close together, as described above, before filling in the neighboring low spot, or you will lock the problem in place.

To fill in low spots, weave back and forth in that area only, remembering to synchronize the weaving direction and the shed. Weave right to left in the stick-shed and left to right in the pull-

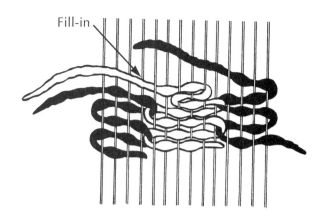

Filling in to correct low spots.

shed. Even good Navajo weavers use fill-ins almost every third row. Fill-ins are a fact of life!

Repairing a Broken Warp

Sometimes a warp thread breaks as you are weaving. How best to repair it depends on where the break is.

When the break is well above the weaving line, use bowline knots (see page 69) to tie a new piece of warp between the broken ends. Be sure the tension of this repaired warp is comparable to that of the other warps.

When the break is at the weaving line, thread a sacking needle with a new piece of warp yarn. Start about 2 inches (5 cm) below the weaving line and follow the course of the broken warp up through the wefts, so that the new and old warps are side by side. Tie the top of the new warp to the end of the broken warp with a bowline knot. Trim the ends to about 1 inch (2.5 cm).

Pull the other end of the new warp out through the back surface of the fabric. Tie it to the lower beam of the loom with a tension comparable to the other warps. As you weave, the weft will cover the knot and its loose ends. When you have finished the weaving, trim off the excess warp on the back of the fabric.

Tiana Bighorse, removing the batten from the loom to change sheds.

One day

as you sit and weave

you may muse on warp and weft:

how they mesh their essences,

how they fuse their strengths.

Warp

so taut

so hard

so straight

so tightly spun

so tightly strung.

Shapes the whole.

Holds the course.

Innerstrength

unseen.

Weft conversely is soft and supple.

Gently yielding.

Textured.

Mellow.

Envelops the warp as it twines.

Buffers the core; creates design.

Thus, as always,

two unite.

Opposites

form a whole—

The basis for creativity;

the foundation

for all of life.

—Halo of the Sun

7 Weaving a Sampler

There's something that makes you hungry, or makes holes in your clothes, or makes you poor. If you leave your batten in your loom, you will think you're this far and when you return you will be less.

—Tiana Bighorse, Tuba City

great and glorious design is in your mind. The warp stretches high and rises further in promise. Fingers long trained by years of work seek their knowing rhythm. The fork, well sanded, fits the hand. The batten glides through warps, spreads them wide to receive the color. Glowing yarns join and create new sensations as they meet. The loom now breathes, has life. Each row is more glorious than the last. Each is compelled by forward progress. Here, indeed, is the joy.

Here is the challenge as well. Will the design in your head fit the warp? Will your colors contrast enough as the weaving grows? Will they contrast too much? Have you dyed enough of each color? But adjustments can always be made as the weaving continues. With this knowing you are now content.

Your hands know their way; they have been here many times before. You settle in to the slow, repetitive work. Designs begin, alter, enlarge, diminish. New colors come. And go. Lulled by these rhythms and visions, the soul takes flight, retracing (not unlike the fingers their patterns) stories told by the Old Ones. Stories of how the Navajo learned to weave. Legends of Spiderwoman. And White Shell Woman. The wisdom they impart.

Your First Weaving

You hold within you the vision of many beautiful Navajo rugs that you have seen. The multiplicity of possibilities is overwhelming. What design shall a first-time weaver undertake?

Traditionally the first weaving a Navajo weaver makes is striped. This is a practical idea as it allows a young girl to get used to a loom and its technicalities. And it removes many of the complications created by a weaver's trying too complicated a design before she is ready. There are lovely first rugs, woven in stripes with many colors. Sometimes each band is a uniform width and the colors vary. Sometimes the bands are of various widths. A well-woven striped rug is a thing of beauty.

Traditional Navajo weavers are endowed with

great patience. They look forward to the many more rugs they will create. They have faith in the future. They can make a striped first rug.

But some weavers may not wish to be traditionally Navajo when choosing their first design. For these weavers, eager to try out everything and anything—preferably all at once—we present a pattern that combines the best of both approaches (shown on page 102).

This sampler has its share of stripes, but also provides the added fun of weaving a design. It can be equally effective woven in bright dramatic colors or in soft plant-dyed hues. The project has been strategically designed with a first-time weaver in mind. For example, the design starts with a band of solid color—when you are cautious and trying to get used to the loom. Then, when you are getting the feeling of the technique and rhythm, the weaving eases first into a vertical, then into a diagonal pattern. By then you may feel you are a virtuoso!

At the center of the weaving is another strategically placed, highly functional stripe; if the bottom design looks like it is too small or too large, this stripe can take up the slack. This stripe also has importance psychologically: It allows you to make great forward strides just when things start slowing down.

From this center stripe onward you are on your own. You can repeat the same design and color scheme of the first half of the sampler if you wish. Or you may want to keep the same design, but change the colors. Or keep the colors and change the design. Or change the design and the colors! In any case, decide on a design for the second half of the sampler that is interesting and challenging so you will be motivated to finish the weaving.

Keep a rough deadline in mind, so that you don't lose your momentum. The finished weaving measures 10 by 23 inches (25 by 58 cm). You should plan on about two weeks to finish the project, depending on how much time you can give to it each day. Tiana Bighorse can complete it in one day and still have time to cook dinner.

Step-by-Step Instructions

First warp the loom (Chapter Five) and tighten the warp. Find and mark the horizontal center (page 85), and mark the center warps to indicate one fourth, one half, and three quarters of the length.

Refer to the chart on page 102 as you weave. All the highlighted numbers and letters in the directions correspond to the diagram.

For weft, this project requires about 8 ounces (227 g) of brown yarn, 4 ounces (113 g) of white yarn, 1/2 ounce (14 g) of orange yarn for the cross, and 2 ounces (57 g) of yellow yarn for the stripes.

❶ First Four Rows

The first four rows of this weaving require special treatment to provide complete coverage of the warp pairs. Push the shed rods up out of the way; you won't need them yet.

Row 1: From right to left, insert a 1-inch (2.5-cm) batten between the warp pairs as follows: in front of the first warp pair, behind the next pair, in front of the next pair, etc. Continue this count of alternating pairs until the batten spans the full width of the warp. The right end of the batten should be in front of the last warp pair. Turn the batten on edge.

Wrap a stick-shuttle with yellow yarn (page 90). From right to left, insert the stick-shuttle in the shed opening just below the batten. With your left hand, grasp the shuttle when it reaches the left side of the warp (see page 103). Pull the shuttle through until the end of the yellow yarn is just inside the right edge of the warp. (This is the same method you will use to lay in new colors later in the weaving process.)

Working from right to left, arrange the yarn in scallops (page 91). Beat the weft securely in place with the fork (page 90). Start at the right

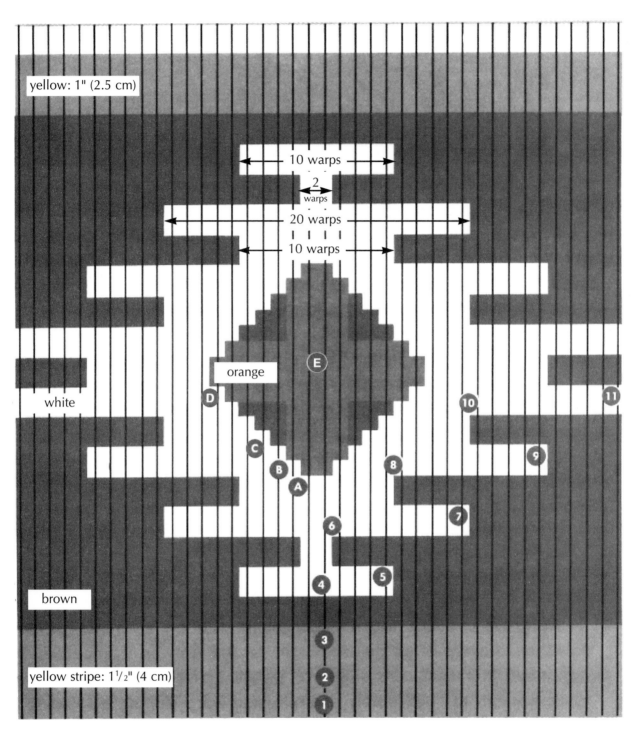

yellow: 1" (2.5 cm)

10 warps

2 warps

20 warps

10 warps

orange

E

white

D

C

B

A

brown

8

10

11

9

7

6

5

4

3

2

1

yellow stripe: 1¹/₂" (4 cm)

Vertical black lines represent forty individual warps. The initial yellow stripe is 1¹/₂ inches (4 cm).
All vertical distances in the white shape are 1/2 inches (1.25 cm).

side of the warp and progress to the left, using a tamping motion. Remove the batten.

Row 2: From right to left, insert the batten between the warp pairs as follows: in back of the first warp pair, in front of the next pair, behind the next pair, etc. When the batten spans the full width of the warp, turn the batten on edge.

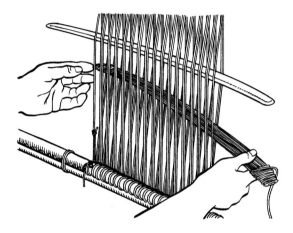

Initial weaving with stick-shuttle between warp pairs, working from right to left.
(Note position of batten on edge.)

Working from left to right, insert the stick-shuttle with yellow yarn through the shed. Pull the shuttle through to the right side, carefully allowing the weft to encircle the outer warp on the left side. Leave the weft loose enough to comfortably encircle the warp without displacing it, but tight enough so as not to create a large loop at the edge. Push the edge loop down with your thumb and finger and arrange the weft in scallops. Beat the weft into place, starting on the left side and working across the weaving line to the right.

Rows 3 and 4 are the same as Rows 1 and 2.

❷ Row 5 and Onward: Regular Sheds
Row 5: The yellow yarn should be hanging from the right side of the warp. Arrange the

shed rods together to create the stick-shed (page 87). Strum the warp (page 86). Insert the batten and turn it on edge. From right to left, insert the stick-shuttle with the yellow weft. Pull the weft through, arrange it in scallops, and beat it into place with the fork.

Row 6: Separate the shed and heddle rods to create the pull-shed (page 87). Strum the warp. Pull the heddle rod. Insert the batten and turn it on edge. Insert the stick-shuttle from left to right. Arrange the weft in scallops and beat it into place.

Repeat Rows 5 and 6 until the yellow stripe is 1½ inches (4 cm) high. Weave in 2 more rows to compensate for packing of the weft. Finish with the yarn at the right side of the warp.

If you run out of yellow yarn while weaving the stripe, rewind the stick-shuttle and continue weaving in the same direction, letting the yarn ends overlap about 1 inch (2.5 cm) (page 90).

❸ Color Change
Check to see if the weaving row is even and that there are no low spots. Fill in the low spots if necessary (page 97). An even row of weaving will insure that the next color will have a straight base.

Break off the yellow yarn about 6 inches (15 cm) from the right edge of the warp. Wrap the stick-shuttle with brown yarn. With the batten in the stick-shed, insert the tail of the yellow yarn into the shed from right to left. Insert the stick-shuttle in the same direction, pulling it through until the end of the brown yarn overlaps the end of the yellow yarn by 1 inch (2.5 cm).

Continue weaving as before, until you have woven a brown stripe 1/2 inch (1 cm) high.

Take stock. Are your edges straight? Measure to be sure the weaving is still 10 inches (25 cm) wide. Is the weaving line straight? Are warp threads showing through the weft? Are warps easing too close together just inside the selvage? If you discover any problems, refer to pages 92 and 96-97 and make corrections now.

Introducing a design with vertical joints

Before beginning your design, you need to decide in which direction and in which shed you will start it. This will be your initial design shed.

Determining the initial design shed

In the first row of a design, the weft must travel from right to left in the shed that places the outer left warp in the forward position (in front of the batten). If you have been following directions, the brown yarn should be at the right edge of the weaving and your batten should be in the stick-shed, which holds the outer left warp forward. Therefore this is your initial design shed. You will start your design right to left in the stick-shed.

If in later weavings you find that when you are beginning a design your last weft is in the initial design shed, then follow these steps to change the direction of the weft:

1. Break off the yarn 1 inch (2.5 cm) inside the right edge of the weaving. Insert the batten in the initial design shed. On the left side of the weaving, lay in the yarn from right to left, so the end of yarn is about 2 inches (5 cm) inside the left edge of the weaving. Pack the yarn.

2. Insert the batten in the alternate shed. Weave from left to right for the entire row. The yarn will now be hanging at the right edge of the weaving. Your next row, worked from right to left, will be the initial design shed in which you will lay in your pattern.

Making vertical hooked joints

The vertical joint used in this sampler is called a hooked joint. It is also known as a weft lock or interlocking weft joint. You may want to learn about other kinds of joints later, but this is a good one to start with. It's the best joint to use when weaving rugs, because it wears better than other joints do.

To make vertical hooked joints, you will need pieces of yarn approximately 15 inches (38 cm) long.

Be sure all the yarns travel in the same direc-

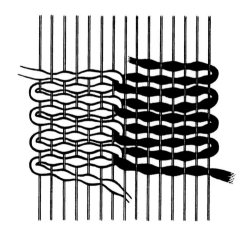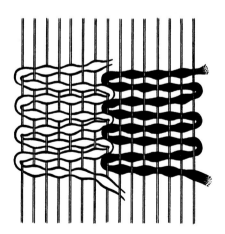

Two types of vertical joints: hooked (left) and turned (right).

Weaving taboo: Don't leave the batten in the loom.

At a ten-day project, women are sitting around the warehouse weaving. I'm sitting next to Tiana's loom, watching her and others weave. One weaver gets up to check the dyepot outside, leaves her batten in the warp on edge. As she reaches the door, another woman notices it, tells others nearby. Then one speaks up, "Nimásání [your grandmother]." There's a round of giggles. The weaver whirls around in the doorway, returns to her loom, removes the batten. Then she turns abruptly in front of her loom and leaves.

tion through each shed or row. When the shed changes, reverse the direction of all the yarns in the next row.

Always start a row with the yarn on the far left, regardless of which direction the row is traveling in or which shed you are in.

Hook yarns only in the pull-shed, weaving from left to right.

Never hook yarns in the stick-shed, weaving from right to left. They are already hooked from the previous row and hooking them again makes an unsightly joint!

Pull the weft tight to make a flat joint, then loosely lay in the weft for the rest of the design area. Do this with each joint, as follows:

1. Insert the weft into the shed. Tug the weft at the joint to pull it securely.

2. With your fingers, press the joint down firmly into place.

3. Loosely lay the yarn in for the rest of the row.

Pressing the joint down after the initial tight tug makes crisp, flat joints. Because joints occur mid-row, you must reach through the warp to grasp the joint between your index finger and thumb in order to slide it down.

❹ Starting the White Pattern Area

(Count: Brown 15, White 10, Brown 15)

Row 1: Set-up: Brown yarn hangs at right edge of the weaving.

1. Insert the batten in the stick-shed (the initial design shed). Count the warps to determine the center 10. Remember, count only those warps that cross the batten. When the center 10 are located, recheck by counting the warps on each side. There should be 15. (Put little pieces of yarn between the warps to mark your place while counting.)

2. Break off the brown yarn about 15 inches (38 cm) from the right edge of the warp. Break off another piece of brown yarn about 15 inches (38 cm) long. From right to left, lay it in behind the 15 warps on the left side of your warp.

3. Break off a 15-inch (38-cm) length of white yarn. Weaving right to left, lay it in behind the center 10 warps.

4. Insert the brown yarn that is hanging at the right edge of the weaving behind the 15 warps on the right side of your warp.

5. Scallop the weft and beat it into place with the fork.

Row 2: Set-up: Three yarns hang from the weaving line—two brown ones with a white in between. All three were woven right to left, so their free ends hang at the left of the design area as shown below. Hook each yarn with its neighbor as follows:

1. Insert the batten in the pull-shed. With your left hand, pick up the brown yarn hanging on the left side of the weaving, and insert it through the shed behind the left 15 warps that cross the batten. Beat it into place. The brown yarn should cross over the adjacent white yarn.

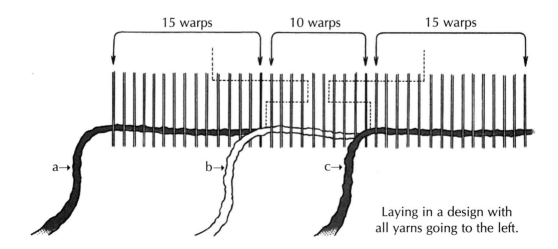

Laying in a design with all yarns going to the left.

106

2. With your left hand, pick up the white yarn underneath the brown, insert it from left to right behind the center 10 warps. Pull it through and beat it into place. As before, the white yarn should cross over the adjacent brown yarn.

12 rows, which will appear as 5 or 6 joints at the edge of the design. When you determine how many rows your weft and packing require to make 1/2 inch (1.25 cm) of weaving, use the same count for each 1/2-inch (1.25-cm) section of the design.

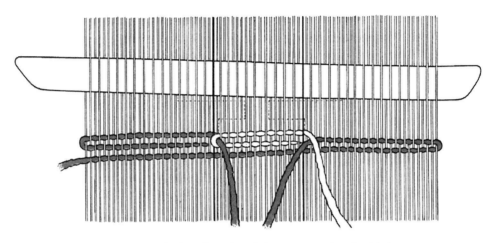

Reversal of weft to the right to create hooked joint.

3. Complete the row with brown yarn. Pick it up from underneath the white and insert it into the shed behind its own 15 warps. Beat it in place. Remember, hooking occurs in the pull-shed only.

Row 3: Set-up: Three yarns hang at the right of the design. Stick-shed.

Starting on the left side of the weaving, left brown yarn travels left (15 warps); white yarn travels left (10 warps); right brown yarn finishes the row (15 warps).

Row 4: Same as Row 2.

Form the design by weaving each color back and forth over its own set of warps. Continue until the white area is slightly more than 1/2 inch (1.25 cm) high—probably a total of 10 or

❺ **Change the Vertical Design**

(New Count: Brown 19, White 2, Brown 19)

When the white area is slightly more than 1/2 inch (1.25 cm) high, decrease the center area of white and expand the side areas of brown.

To change vertical designs:

Only decrease or advance the count in one direction at a time.

It takes two rows (one to the left, then one to the right) to set up a design change.

Row 1: Set-up: Three yarns hang at right of the design. Stick-shed.

1. Weave the left brown yarn to left edge behind 15 warps.

2. Weave the white yarn to the left for 6 warps.

3. Weave the right brown yarn to the left for 19

Vena with her first weaving.

You don't have to have the nanoolzhee' *[warp] up in four days. You just have to do something toward the next rug—like set a bag of wool aside, or start spinning the* nanoolzhee' *[warp], or look and see what new colors you will need, or think about what the next design will be.*

—Navajo weaver, Tuba City

warps. (This count is 4 beyond the previous 15; there will be 2 wefts in the same shed for 4 warps.)

Row 2: Set-up: Three yarns hang at the left of the design. Pull-shed.

1. Weave the left brown yarn to the left behind 19 warps (4 past the previous 15). Hook the brown yarn with the adjacent white yarn.

2. Weave the white yarn to the right for 2 warps. Hook it with the brown that it meets there.

3. Weave the right brown yarn to the right edge for 19 warps.

The new count is now established. Continue weaving for 1/2 inch (1.25 cm).

❻ Change the Vertical Design

(New Count: Brown 10, White 20, Brown 10)
When the white area is slightly more than 1 inch (2.5 cm) high, change the design again.

Remember, it takes two rows (one to the left, then one back to the right) to set up a design change.

Row 1: Set-up: Three yarns hang at the right of the design. Stick-shed.

1. Weave the left brown yarn to the left edge behind 19 warps.

2. Weave the white yarn to the left for 11 warps (9 beyond the 2). The white yarn will be on top of the brown yarn in the same shed for 9 warps.

3. Weave the right brown yarn to the left for 10 warps.

Row 2: Set-up: Three yarns hang at the left of the design. Pull-shed.

1. Weave the left brown yarn to the right for 10 warps; hook it with the white yarn.

2. Weave the white yarn to the right for 20 warps; hook it with the brown yarn.

3. Weave the right brown yarn to the right edge, behind 10 warps.

The new count is now established. Continue weaving for 1/2 inch (1.25 cm).

❼ Change the Vertical Design
(New Count: Brown 15, White 10, Brown 15)
Row 1: Set-up: The white area is slightly more than 1½ inches (4 cm) high. Three yarns hang at the right of the design. Stick-shed.

1. Weave the left brown yarn to the left edge behind 10 warps.

2. Weave the white yarn 15 warps to the left (5 fewer than in the previous row).

3. Weave the right brown yarn 15 warps to the left (5 more than in the previous row).

Row 2: Set-up: Three yarns hang at the left of the design. Pull-shed.

1. Weave the left brown yarn 15 warps to the right; hook it with the white yarn.

2. Weave the white yarn 10 warps to the right; hook it with the brown yarn.

3. Weave the right brown yarn to the right edge, to complete the row.

Continue weaving for 1/2 inch (1 cm).

❽ Change the Vertical Design
(New Count: Brown 5, White 30, Brown 5)
Row 1: Set-up: Three yarns hang at the right of the design. Stick-shed.

1. Weave the left brown yarn 15 warps to the left.

2. Weave the white yarn 20 warps to the left.

3. Weave the right brown yarn 5 warps to the left.

Row 2: Set-up: Three yarns hang at the left of the design. Pull-shed.

1. Weave the left brown yarn 5 warps to the right; hook it with the white.

2. Weave the white yarn 30 warps to the right; hook it with the brown.

3. Weave the right brown yarn 5 warps to the right edge.

This count will continue for 1/2 inch (1.25 cm), but stop here and take stock before continuing to the next row, which begins the center diamond design. You are now at point ⒶÍin the chart.

You have now completed slightly more than 4 inches (10 cm) of your weaving. If you have found the techniques difficult and would like more time to master the vertical designs, omit the center diamond and continue weaving only the large white shape, as described below in the section "Completion of the large white design." When you have finished weaving the second half of the rug, turn to "Finishing the Rug" on page 116.

If you are pleased with your results so far and are eager for more of a challenge, skip the instructions below for completing the large white design and instead begin with the section called "Weaving the center diamond." There are considerable differences in the ways people weave—for example, some people pack harder than others, some use heavier yarn. So we will give you measurements for the diamond, but will not specify its exact placement within the white shape.

Completion of the large white design

❾ When you get to number **❾** on the chart, reduce the white shape by 5 warps on each side, for 1/2 inch (1.25 cm). The white shape will have the same boundaries as it did at number **❻**.

❿ When you get to number **❿**, expand the white area to the edges of the weaving; the brown yarns will be temporarily discontinued. Break the brown yarns off about 1 inch (2.5 cm) from the weaving and tuck the ends in under the white yarn as you continue weaving. Continue this part of the design for 1/2 inch (1.25 cm).

⓫ At number **⓫**, lay the brown yarn in again and weave it for 5 warps on each side, just as you did at number **❾**. Within this block of color, you will reach the middle of the design (about 5¾ inches [15 cm] from the beginning). Now you can begin to reverse the design.

Weaving the center diamond (a diagonal pattern)

There are many ways to weave a diagonal pattern. The technique you select is based on how steep an angle your design requires, as well as how strong a joint is needed. We have chosen the square diamond with the stepped edge for the sampler. We will use the hooked joint, as it provides the greatest strength.

The stepped edge on the square diamond is made with the same technique that you have been using to make vertical hooked joints. Each step is only 1/4 inch (6 mm) high.

To form the diamond, first expand and then decrease your count consistently (see below). To begin, expand to the left, then to the right, just as you have been doing in the white area. After 2 expansion rows, weave 2 rows in place. A total of 4 or more rows constitutes one step. If your yarn is thin and 4 rows do not make 1/4

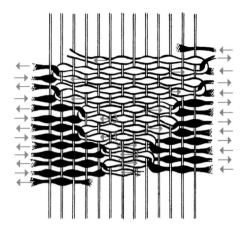

Detail of hooked wefts in stepped-edge diamond. Arrows show weaving direction.

inch (6 mm), weave additional rows to reach this height.

Ⓐ Laying in the First Step of the Diamond
(Diamond count: Orange 2)
Row 1: Set-up: Three yarn ends hang at the right of the design. Stick-shed.

1. Weave the left brown yarn to the left edge.

2. Break off a piece of white yarn. Lay it (right to left) behind the next 14 warps. (It will begin just left of the 2 center warps and will continue to the edge of the white.)

3. Break off a piece of orange yarn. Lay it in (right to left) behind the 2 center warps.

4. Weave the existing white yarn up to the beginning of the orange yarn.

5. Weave the final brown yarn 5 warps to the left, where the white yarn will meet it on the return row.

Row 2: Set-up: Five yarn ends hang at the left of the design. Pull-shed.

Reaching through the warp to pull weft through shed.

Maybe your deceased sister or aunt or grandmother might be watching and wanting to help you and when you leave the loom they might weave on it and that would be bad luck. You might never finish the rug, or you might get sore arms, or go blind. Or your warp threads might break whenever you try to string the loom. So when someone leaves it [the batten] in the loom, they tell them "Nimásání," ("Your grandmother is watching")—and they just know what it means.

—Navajo weaver, Tuba City

1. Weave the brown yarn to the right; hook it with the white yarn.

2. Weave the white yarn to the right; hook it with the orange yarn.

3. Weave the orange yarn to the right; hook it with the white yarn.

4. Weave the white to the right; hook it with the brown yarn.

5. Weave the brown yarn to the right edge.

Continue with the same count until the step is 1/4 inch (6 mm) high.

Ⓑ **Laying in the Second Step of the Diamond**
(Diamond count: Orange 4)
Row 1: Set-up: Five yarn ends hang at the right of the design. Stick-shed.

1. Weave the left brown yarn to the left edge.

2. Weave the white yarn to the left.

3. Weave the orange yarn to the left for 3 warps.

4. Weave the right white yarn to the orange yarn, less one warp.

5. Weave the brown yarn to the left to the white yarn.

Row 2: Set-up: Five yarn ends hang at the left of the design. Pull-shed.

1. Weave the left brown yarn to the right; hook it with the white yarn.

2. Weave the white yarn to the right; hook it with the orange yarn.

3. Weave the orange yarn to the right for 4 warps; hook it with the white yarn.

4. Weave the white yarn to the right; hook it with the brown yarn.

5. Weave the brown yarn to the right edge.

Continue with the same count until the step is 1/4 inch (6 mm) high.

Continuing the stepped edge of the diamond

When each step is 4 rows or 1/4 inch (6 mm) high, expand the diamond one warp on each side. You will do this twice. Your count will be four.

In the first row, remember to weave the yarns from right to left in the stick-shed. Weave the orange yarn one warp farther than in the previous row. Weave the right white yarn one warp less than in the previous row.

On the second row, weave the yarns from left to right in the pull-shed. The left white yarn and the orange yarn hook when they meet. The orange yarn travels to meet the right white yarn, and they hook.

As you work the diamond, weave the brown and white background pattern as shown at numbers ❾, ❿, and ⓫ on the chart.

Ⓖ **Laying in the Remaining Steps of the Diamond**

(Diamond count: Brown 1, Orange 4, Brown 1)

The orange area is now 4 warps wide, which is the full width of the base of the cross in the center of the design. The base will remain at this width for about the next inch (2.5 cm) of weaving. You will now begin the brown background, which will continue the diagonal steps begun with the orange yarn. Adding the brown background expands the diamond by 1 warp on each side.

Row 1: Set-up: Five yarn ends hang at the right of the design. Stick-shed.

1. Weave the left brown yarn to the left edge.

2. Weave the white yarn to the left to continue the white design.

3. Lay in a new brown yarn behind the warp to the left of the orange area. (Counting warps from the left side of the weaving, this would be warp number 18.) Anchor the tapered end of the brown yarn by winding it counterclockwise twice around the warp.

4. Weave the orange yarn to the left for 4 warps.

5. Lay in another brown yarn behind the warp to the right of the orange area. (Counting warps from the right side of the weaving, this would be warp number 18.) Anchor the end of the yarn as you did in Step 3.

6. Weave the white yarn to the left to meet the new brown yarn.

7. Weave the brown yarn to the left to the edge of the white design.

Row 2: Set-up: Seven yarns hang at the left of their designs. Pull-shed.

1. Weave the left brown yarn to the right. Hook it with the white yarn.

2. Weave the new brown yarn to the right for 1 warp. Hook it with the orange yarn.

3. Weave the orange yarn to the right for 4 warps. Hook it with the brown yarn.

4. Weave the brown yarn to the right for 1 warp. Hook it with the white yarn.

5. Weave the white yarn to the right. Hook it with the brown yarn.

6. Weave the brown yarn to the right edge of the weaving.

7. Weave two more rows so that the design is 4 rows or 1/4 inch (6 mm). Continue the stepped edge of the design by expanding the diamond 1 warp on each side.

Row 1: The yarns will travel right to left in the stick-shed. Increase left diamond yarn 1 warp to the left. Decrease right white yarn 1 warp to left.

Row 2: The yarns will travel left to right in the pull-shed. Decrease the left white yarn 1 warp to the left. Increase right diamond yarn 1 warp to the right.

Continue making steps until you are about 3/8 inch (9 mm) from the middle of the design. Do not forget to extend the white area to the edge of the weaving when you reach number ❿ on the chart.

Discontinuing the Brown Background

You will temporarily discontinue the brown background yarns at the edges of the design. Break the left brown yarn, leaving a 1-inch (2.5 -cm) wispy end. Weave the wisp end to the left. Weave the next white yarn to the left edge over the brown wisp end. When you have woven to the right side of the weaving,

break the brown yarn at the right edge before you weave it to the left.

◑ **Extending the Arms of the Cross**

About 3/8 inch (9 mm) below the vertical center of your design, you will extend the arms of the cross, which will add another step to the diamond.

Row 1: Temporarily discontinue using the left brown diamond yarn. Break it off 1 inch (2.5 cm) from the weaving and insert it in the stick-shed. Weave the white yarn to the left edge of the weaving.

Weave the orange yarn 1 warp beyond the brown area to establish a new step. Weave the remaining brown yarn as usual.

Weave the last white yarn 1 warp short of the edge of the brown area of the diamond.

Row 2: Discontinue the remaining brown yarn. Break it off 1 inch (2.5 cm) from the weaving and insert it in the pull-shed.

Begin the row at left. Weave the white yarn from left to right to meet the orange yarn. The orange yarn travels 1 warp beyond the edge of the brown design area to make a new step. Hook the orange yarn with the white yarn. Weave the white yarn to complete the row.

At the end of this row, you will have three yarns hanging from the weaving.

Repeat the process to weave Rows 3 and 4. When these rows are complete, expand the diamond one warp in each direction to complete the final step of the diamond.

Continue weaving. When you are 1/4 inch (6 mm) below the vertical center, add brown yarn to the edges across 5 warps.

◉ **The Middle of the Design**

When you reach the first vertical mark on the warp, you will have completed one fourth of your weaving. When finishing the design, consult the chart and the first half of your design to determine count. The second half of the design will proceed much more quickly—you will be more certain of the process and will need to refer to the directions less frequently, or perhaps not at all.

How to decrease steps and finish the diamond

Row 1: Weave the yarns right to left in the stick-shed. Decrease the left diamond yarn one warp to left. Increase the right white yarn one warp to the left.

Row 2: Weave the yarns from left to right in the pull-shed. The left white yarn travels one more warp to meet the diamond yarn. The right diamond yarn meets the right white yarn by traveling one warp less.

Alternate rows until you have completed the top half of the diamond.

Finishing the Rug

Days and months have passed since that grand beginning. Continual interruptions have interplayed with your warp. But now you are approaching the end and you know it. Not only is there a mounting excitement within you. Not only can you see the whole of your design beginning and reversing and fitting together. But there is also a certain weariness you feel each day even before you begin to weave. The remaining space has become smaller and tighter and slower. The weaving that once showed progress minute by minute now seems to require an eternity row for row. You have graduated to your finest batten, and it is too big for the space. You pull forth your sacking needle in its stead. Over-one-warp, under-one-warp, over-one-warp, under-one-warp, you needle-weave each weft. Inside you know how many days it will take to complete this final inch. You know as well that there is no way to hurry the pace. You recall how in your youth you complained of the tedious finishing, of the cramped back and the aching muscles. You vowed you would never weave another rug! Muscles ache even more now that you are older. But you do not think of complaint. You know there will be another. And another.

The Second Half of the Weaving: The Countdown

The second half of the weaving will proceed much as before, but the weaving space becomes smaller and smaller. To finish, you'll need some of the smaller weaving tools. Persevere. Remember that Navajo rugs have been woven this way for centuries. It is possible!

1. When you are 9 or 10 inches (23 or 25 cm) from the top of the weaving, change to your 1/2-inch (1.25-cm) batten. Because space is at a premium, keep the shed rods up out of the way of the fork as far as possible.

2. When there isn't room in a shed to insert your fingers, use a 6-inch (15-cm) stick with a broken end as a mini-shuttle. Take the yarns one at a time. Twirl the broken end of the stick into the wispy end of the yarn and poke it through the shed.

3. At some point, you will no longer be able to tamp the weft into position in the regular way because the tines of the fork will hit the shed rods. To pack the weft, you now have to bear down on the fork instead. When pressing with the fork, facile Navajo weavers usually lead with the edge of the fork that is nearest the bound end of the weft. Then they rotate the tines to press with the other edge. Moving across the weaving row with this rocking motion, the weaver can insert ample weft in a tight spot.

My grandmother told me when I first started weaving, never to leave the bee ník'í'níltlish [batten] in the loom. She said that a long time ago, a weaver did that, and when she was outside she heard a sound inside, and it was the sound of something weaving, and she went inside and there was nothing there. So that's why you should never leave it in there.

—Navajo weaver, Tuba City

4. When you have 4 inches (10 cm) left to weave, change to an even smaller batten. If you do not have one, remove the upper shed rod, refine its point, and use it instead.

5. When you have 2 inches (5 cm) left to weave, if you still have the upper shed rod in place, remove it. You now have only the heddle rod to open a shed. To create the stick-shed, thread a small batten through alternate warps. Insert yarn into the shed with an umbrella rib or sacking needle, depending on the design.

   An umbrella rib may be used as an over-sized needle and is especially useful when weaving a solid stripe. If the eye is large enough, thread the weft. If not, thread a fine string through the eye, tie it in a loop, and use the loop as an eye for threading the weft.

6. Once you have begun the final stripe, you can change to a new technique to make the weaving easier:

   Weave in the top 4 rows as you did the first 4, traveling under and over each pair of warps. After you have woven each row, push the weft up to the top of the weaving.

   After the top 4 rows are in place, thread a batten over and under alternate warps. Once the batten is in position, weave 2 wefts in the shed: one row above the batten, which you will push up to join the top rows, and one row beneath the batten, which you will push down to the weaving line (see drawing on page 118).

   When these wefts are packed in place, remove the batten and thread it through the alternate shed, and again weave 2 wefts.

   When the heddle rod is of no more use, remove it by sliding the rod from the loops and pulling the string out.

7. Eventually you will not be able to insert a

117

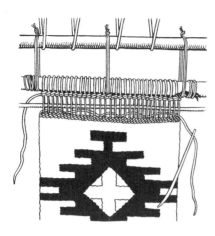

Utilizing batten to weave two wefts.

batten at all. At this point use the sacking needle, packing the weft as firmly as possible with the fork. Keep weaving in wefts until you are certain that you cannot insert another. Then insert the tines of the fork between rows of weft and pack the last inch (2.5 cm) of weaving down even more firmly. This will probably open up a little more space.

8. Once again, insert as many wefts as you can. Again you will come to the point where you are absolutely positive you cannot insert another row. At this point force in 4 more wefts. Slowly and painstakingly thread your weft through the warp with the sacking needle, being careful not to split warps or cross weft. Blunt the point of the needle if necessary.

If you were a Navajo weaver selling your weaving to a trading post, the trader would try to tell which end you started with and which you finished with. Do not let the finished end be thinner. The warps should not show through the weft. The packing should be so tight that if the trader forced his fingernail into the fabric, it could not be felt on the reverse side. Force the remaining wefts in place, and you are finished.

Remove the Weaving from the Loom

Now remove the sampler from the loom.

1. Loosen and remove the top rope.

2. Untie the twine around the dowels.

3. Remove the twine binding from the two dowels.

4. Untie the ends of the edging cords from the dowels.

Your weaving is complete. You can use it flat on the table or hang it on the wall. Or you can double it to make a purse or bag for your weaving tools or knitting paraphernalia. Or how about a book bag? Or a medicine pouch? Smoke-pouch? Saddlebag?

To Make a Purse or Bag

Doubled, the dimensions of the weaving are about 10 inches (25 cm) wide and 11½ inches (29 cm) deep. The purse or bag can be secured at the top by a Navajo button and loop, or lined with cotton and zippered. A woven or braided shoulder strap or handle makes it easy to carry. You can also add decorative embellishments to the bag.

Straps and Handles

Design the strap or handle to suit the purpose of the bag. A handle long enough to extend along the sides gives a purse added body and style. A strap on a tool bag or medicine pouch, to be worn diagonally across the body, needs additional length. A smoke-pouch would not need

118

Don't leave the batten in the loom. "Something" might come along and unravel it when you're not there. It's like the spirits of the things that work against you.

—Navajo weaver, Tuba City

any handle; a knapsack may require two—one on each side to slip your arms through.

The straps or handles may be woven or braided. If they are woven, they will be wider than if they are braided.

Attaching a woven strap or handle

The strap or handle can be woven on an inkle loom or a rigid-heddle loom. A good width is 1½ inches (4 cm). The width of the woven strap or handle makes it easier to open the bag and gain access to its contents.

To sew the handle to the bag, fold the weaving in half and attach one end of the strap at the fold. With weft thread and the sacking needle, stitch the sides of the weaving along the handle with a running stitch, alternately picking up a few wefts from the weaving and a few from the strap. Make some extra stitches where the handle is attached to the opening of the bag for reinforcement.

Attach the other end of the handle to the fold at the other side of the bag, then stitch it in the same way.

Attaching a braided strap or handle

A braided strap or handle is faster to make than a woven one, and its roundness feels good to the hand. You don't need a loom or special equipment.

Measure how long you want the finished strap or handle to be. Braid lengths of yarn at least three times that long—or longer if you want to add tassels at the ends.

To attach the braided strap or handle, fold the weaving in half and sew the sides together. Then stitch the handle to the purse along this seam.

Fasteners

You can use a variety of fasteners to close the purse or bag you've made. The simplest is a loop stitched to the back that slips over a button stitched to the front. Or you can install a cotton lining—with or without inside pockets—and add a zipper.

Embellishments

You may want to personalize your bag—add your own kind of trim or fringe. Use the weaving as a canvas and let your imagination go!

Add buttons—old Navajo tarnished silver

Grace Homer, at the loom.

On the day that you finish your rug, you are not supposed to start another one. But within four days, you are supposed to string up the nanoolzhee' [warp] for the next one.

—Navajo weaver, Tuba City

buttons, organic buttons, any that suit your taste. Sew them around the opening of the bag, incorporate them into the design, attach them at intervals along the handle, reminiscent of old Navajo medicine pouches.

Think Forward

You may think of this as a time of completion. Or a time of beginning. In either case, remember the wisdom of the loom: You have four days to begin your next weaving—a day for East, a day for South, a day for West, a day for North.

Rewarp the loom, spin yarn, collect dye plants, plan the design. For four days after your weaving is completed, think forward toward the next.

And may the next weaving be ever better.

You shouldn't take too long to finish your rug or you might get sick.

There was a lady and she was weaving a saddle blanket. And every time they looked at it, it was just the same (indicating about two feet from the floor). And she would work on it and it wouldn't change much. And it was there a long time and she got sick. So they took her to a medicine man and he said that the rug was making her sick and so her son just took the rug and cut it off at the top and took it behind a hill to get rid of it.

But then, as he stood behind the hill, he looked at it and he thought about how much he needed a saddle blanket, and so he strung it up again and finished it himself, so he could use it.

So this is what they mean, that if you have a rug and it takes you two or three years to finish it, then that will make you sick. That's just what they say.

—Navajo weaver, Shonto

Weaver pulling binding cord to remove finished rug from loom.

8 Advanced Techniques

When you're making a good rug for the floor, join all the yarns like this [interlocking weft]. Diagonals, too; don't just go around the same warp. If you just weave something to put on the wall, it doesn't matter. The other way [interlocking warp] is okay.

—Tiana Bighorse, Tuba City

For many years I taught Navajo weaving at the University of New Mexico in Gallup, a small town bordering the Navajo Nation. In one class on advanced techniques, a Navajo student, Ella Begay, claiming to be a novice, simply sat at her loom and began weaving flawlessly. She had spent her childhood watching her mother at the loom. The rhythm was in her heart long before her hands learned the way.

In this class I intended to teach a sampler of complex weaving joints and styles. Students would begin a new technique each week and complete several inches at home. Class One covered the turned joint. Ella returned to Class Two with her sampler section complete and an entire rug woven in that technique. To Class Three, she brought a rug combining hooked and turned joints.

She explained that her mother had always wanted to learn some of the complicated tech-niques, but no one would teach her. One day, years ago, her mother had visited a relative who was a proficient weaver and asked if she would show her. Give me all your sheep, then I'll teach you, the relative had said.

"So, I never learned how—until now."

Triple Side and End Selvage Cords

Selvage cords increase the durability of weavings that are exposed to edge wear (such as saddle blankets and floor rugs). Some weavers add selvage cords simply for their appearance: They add color or texture and create fuller tassels at the corners.

There are double as well as triple selvage cords. Triple selvage cords are more decorative and durable. They have the appearance of a continuous twining along the edge of the weaving.

There are several ways to incorporate side selvage cords into your weaving. The method we use is best for maintaining straight edges. One two-ply strand of tripled selvage cord is included with the edge warp for about every 6 turns of the weft (12 rows).

To make a triple edging cord for the ends of the weaving, rotate three instead of two strands while twining warp turns (see page 73).

Materials

A length of 2-ply cord (page 58), six times the length of the weaving plus 60 inches (152 cm): Cut the cord into six strands, each the length of the weaving plus 10 inches (25 cm).

Installing Selvage Cords

After the warp is fastened to the loom and the shed rods have been positioned:

1. Tie three 2-ply cords together with an overhand knot, 5 inches (13 cm) from the ends of the cords. Bind the 5-inch (13-cm) section to the bottom dowel, left of the warp. (When the weaving is complete, you will tie this 5-inch [13-cm] section to the edging cords at the end of the weaving to form a five- or six-strand tassel.)

2. Pass the cords behind the shed rods and up to the top dowel. Wrap the cords twice around the dowel and slip the end through the wrapping. The tension should be snug, but not as tight as the warp.

3. Repeat this process on the right side of the warp with three more 2-ply cords.

Incorporating Cords While Weaving

Place one strand of each triple selvage cord in front of the upper shed rod. The strands in front of the shed rod will be woven with the edge warp.

Row 1: As you insert the batten into the stick-shed, pick up the forward selvage strand on the left side of the warp. Lay in weft from right to left. On the left edge, the weft will pass behind one selvage strand and in front of two.

Row 2: With the batten, pick up the forward strand of selvage cord on the right side of the warp and insert the batten into the pull-shed. On the left side, leave the selvage strands behind the batten. Lay in weft from left to right. The weft will turn around one selvage strand on the left side, and travel behind one selvage strand on the right side.

Repeat Rows 1 and 2. Continue weaving for a total of 12 rows. One strand of each edging cord will have 6 weft turns on it.

Now you are ready to twist the selvage cords. On one edge of the weaving, remove the bound selvage strand from in front of the shed rod by sliding the rod to the side. Reach between the bound selvage strand and the edge warp. Grasp a free edging strand and pull it through. Place that strand in front of the upper shed rod to hold it forward. Slide the rod back. Repeat the same process on the other edge.

Continue weaving, binding this new strand to the edge warp as before. After you have woven 12 rows (6 weft turns), rotate the strands again, bringing the third, unbound strand forward.

Throughout the weaving there will always be 2 strands bound together by the weft: one edge warp and one of the selvage strands. There will always be two unbound selvage strands, which provide a visible and functional edging. The three strands of each cord are rotated successively in the same order. Be careful that you bring the correct strand forward each time.

A continually increasing twist will develop above the shed rod. After a while, untie the tops of the selvage cords, untwist them, and retie them.

You know when you need the ceremony if your arm aches (the one you use all the time for the batten), or if you're tired all the time, or if you start not seeing too well. Then you know it's because you have been weaving too much.

—Tiana Bighorse, Tuba City

The Inversion Technique

Most Navajo rugs are designed with solid stripes at the beginning and end of the rug to simplify the weaving of the final, tedious 2 inches (5 cm). An alternative to finishing a weaving at the top is completing it in the center. This is especially appropriate when the design has a simpler center, as do saddle blankets with ornate borders.

1. First weave upward from the bottom to the beginning of the solid center section.

2. Remove dowels Nos. 1 and 2 from the loom and invert the weaving, being certain to tie the shed rods together. Remount the weaving and tighten the warp.

3. Invert the upper shed/heddle arrangement by inserting your batten next to the shed rod in its now lower position. Turn the batten on edge. Remove the rod and place it in the opening above the heddles. Remove the batten.

4. You are now ready to resume weaving. First weave your four rows to correspond to the usual first four rows of weaving (over and under pairs). Continue weaving using the same sheds you did before.

5. Finish the rug as usual, packing as many wefts as possible into the center of the rug.

The "Up-and-Over" Technique

When weaving a rug that is longer than the height of the loom, use the "up-and-over" technique. This method requires sturdier beams and mountings and is more difficult to tighten, so we do not recommend it for beginners.

The directions here require converting the loom described in Chapter Four. See pages 63, 65, and 129, and the drawing on page 128.

Materials and tools

- 1/2-inch (2-cm) metal pipe, 36 inches (91 cm) long

126

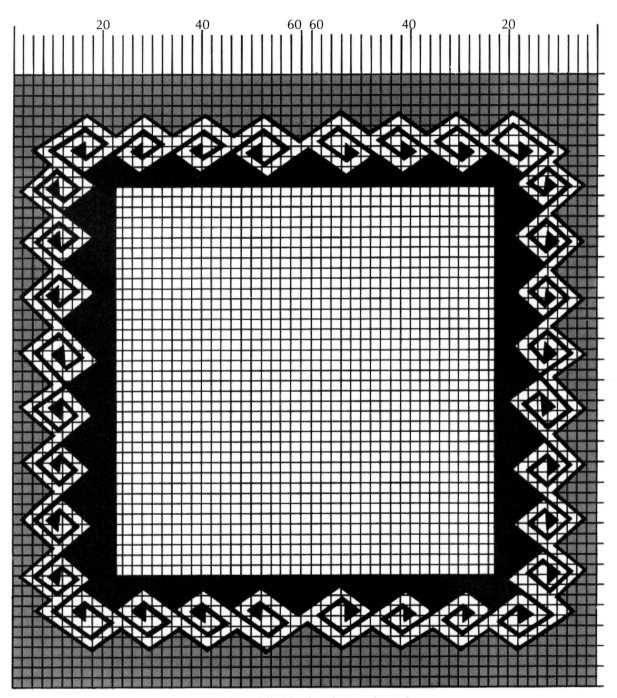

Single saddle blanket design charted.

Weft required: 2½ lbs. (1 kg)
☐ White: 1½ lb. (680 g)
■ Black: 1/2 lb. (227 g)
■ Grey: 1/2 lb. (227 g)
(red or ochre)

Size 30 by 30 inches (76 by 76 cm)
*Warp required: 500 yards (457 m)
*Warping particulars:

Dowel 1 = 121 markers
Dowel 2 = 120 markers
Warping frame nails:
28½ inches (72 cm) apart

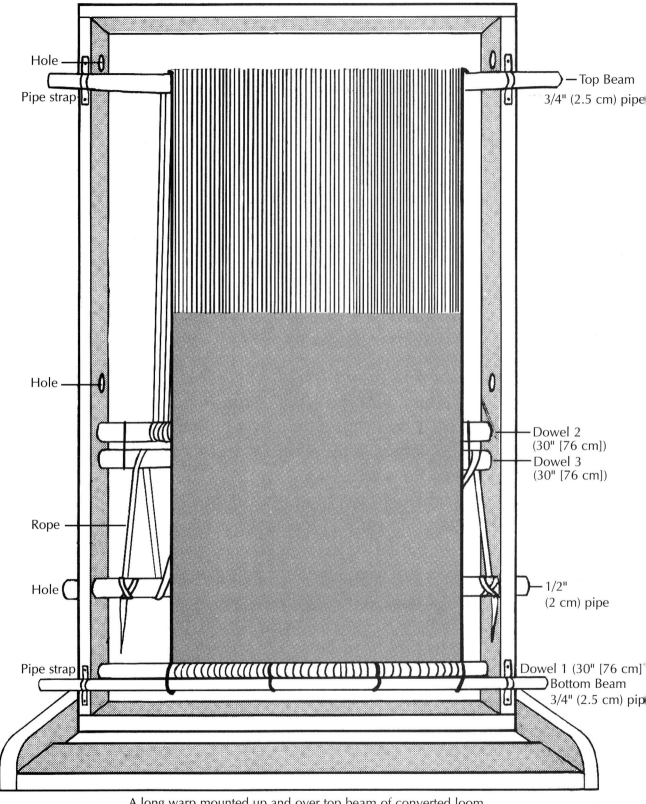

Hole

Pipe strap

Hole

Rope

Hole

Pipe strap

Top Beam
3/4" (2.5 cm) pipe

Dowel 2
(30" [76 cm])

Dowel 3
(30" [76 cm])

1/2"
(2 cm) pipe

Dowel 1 (30" [76 cm]
Bottom Beam
3/4" (2.5 cm) pip

A long warp mounted up and over top beam of converted loom.

- 2 3/4-inch (2.5-cm) metal pipes, 36 inches (91 cm) long
- 3 1-inch (2.5-cm) dowels, 30 inches (76 cm) long
- 4 pipe straps: for mounting 3/4-inch (2.5-cm) pipe. If you used pipe straps before, reuse them here.
- screws
- strong baling wire
- drill with 7/8-inch (22-mm) wood bit
- screwdriver

How to convert the loom

1. Replace the top and bottom beams with the 3/4-inch (2.5-cm) pipe. Mount the pipe with the pipe straps.

2. Drill three 7/8-inch (22-mm) holes in both uprights of loom. Position the holes 12 inches (30.5 cm), 24 inches (61 cm), and 40 inches (102 cm) from the base. The spacing of these holes will accommodate a variety of weaving sizes.

How to warp the converted loom

Prepare your warp (Chapter Five) on 30-inch (76-cm) dowels, short enough to fit inside the loom frame.

1. Wire dowel No. 1 (with the knotted warp ends) to the bottom pipe beam at 7-inch (18-cm) intervals. Turn the sharp wire ends away from you.

2. Raise dowel No. 2 up and over the top beam, and let it hang inside the loom frame.

3. Wire dowels Nos. 2 and 3 together at 7-inch (18-cm) intervals, using a spacer to keep the intervals a consistent 1 inch (2.5 cm) apart. Turn the sharp wire ends away from you.

4. The final step is attaching and tightening the rope. Where you will position the pipe on which to wind the rope depends on your warp length. Stand behind the loom and position the 1/2-inch (2-cm) pipe in whatever hole is closest to dowel No. 3, allowing at least 5 inches (13 cm) between the pipe and the dowel. Then wind the rope around dowel No. 3 and the 1/2-inch (2-cm) pipe; use an over-and-away, under-and-toward, left-to-right direction when winding. Cinch the rope to tighten it, progressing right to left.

Muscle up and bear down! You will be tired before it's tight!

Rolling the rug under as the weaving progresses

The timing and distances will vary depending on the length of your warp, but here are some rough guidelines that apply to a warp about 40 inches (102 cm) long.

1. When you have woven about 20 inches (51 cm), release the weaving by removing the tensioning rope and the wires that connect dowel No. 1 to the bottom beam.

2. Move the 1/2-inch (2-cm) pipe to the center hole. Pull the weaving under the bottom beam and wire dowel No. 1 to the 1/2-inch (2-cm) pipe.

3. Attach dowel No. 3 to the top beam with the rope in the usual way (page 78).

Hooked and Turned Joints

There are basically two kinds of vertical joints: hooked and turned (page 104). The hooked joint is also called the interlocking weft joint. This joint creates a pattern when two wefts hook each other; the joint occurs between warps.

Grace Homer, finishing a big rug mounted with the up-and-over technique.

The turned joint is also called a shared warp joint or interlocking warp joint. This joint creates a pattern when two wefts alternately turn around the same warp; the joint occurs on a warp.

There are advantages and disadvantages to each joint. The hooked joint is more difficult to make flat. But, because the joint occurs between the warps, there is less weft build-up when weaving long verticals (such as in a border) so it requires fewer fill-ins. In a turned joint, weft builds up because there are 4 wefts and 1 warp at each intersection instead of just 2 wefts.

Durability is another matter. Tiana will not use the turned joint in a weaving that is intended for floor use; rugs made with the turned joint do not hold up well.

When I directed the Navajo Weaving Restoration Center, I had the opportunity to examine numerous old textiles that had both types of joints. I noticed that the rugs with turned joints had excessive warp breakage. The turning warps wrapped by multiple wefts tended to wear and break. The reason for this is that the multiple wefts wear on the single warp every time the rug is moved—or shaken! Once a turning warp breaks, the freed weft loops curl up and wear away, and expose the adjacent warps to additional wear, too. It's just a matter of time before there's a large hole.

Based on my restoration experience, I conclude that the best use for the turned joint is for rendering a smooth diagonal line in a wall hanging.

Rugs with the hooked joint showed no warp breakage at the joints. Because hooked wefts interlock between warps, there is no pressure on the warp. Also, if a warp does break for any reason, the interlocking weft loops of the hooked joints remain flat and in place, protecting adjoining warps and maintaining the integrity of the fabric.

Perfecting the hooked joint

If you enjoy making hooked joints, or if you want a durable weaving that depends on the strength of the hooked joint, consider weaving one of the following two designs.

Each contains only vertical lines. Warp and weft computations, warping dimensions, and design counts are provided next to the charts. Follow the basic directions for making hooked joints on pages 104–105.

The Greek Key: The scrollwork in this design, charted on page 132, is characteristic of rugs from the Old Crystal trading post, which incorporated Persian designs.

Two Grey Hills: This design, charted on page 133, is characteristic of the eastern Two Grey Hills area of the Navajo Nation. This area is admired for its fine tapestry weave, which uses natural fleece hues.

Perfecting the turned joint

In the turned joint, two wefts turn around and share the same turning warp (as shown below). Here are some guidelines and tips to remember.

1. Counting the turned joint: With the turned joint, each individual warp is counted and used. This differs from the hooked joint, in which only those warps crossing the batten are counted and used.

   Throughout the instructions for turned joints, each individual warp is assigned a number followed by L or R, denoting its position on the left or right of the weaving.

Two wefts circling a turning warp.

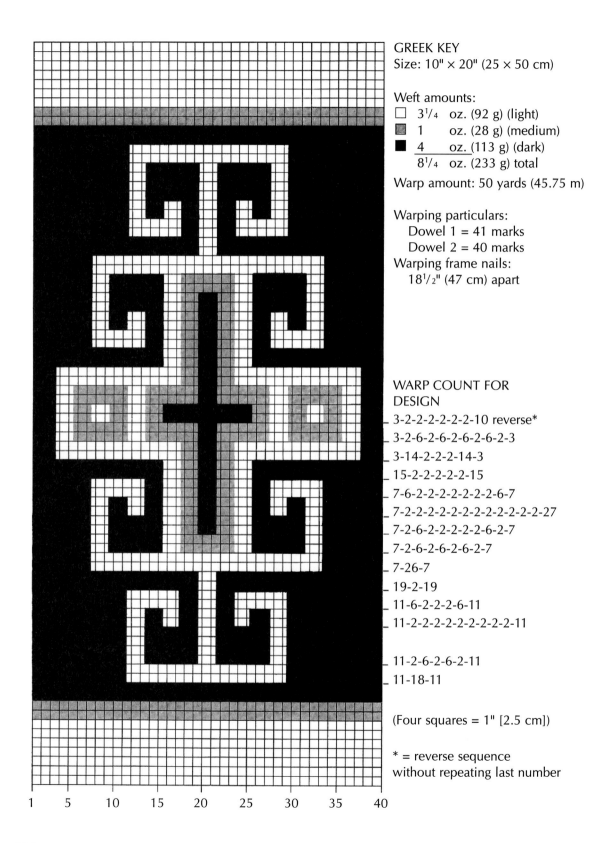

GREEK KEY
Size: 10" × 20" (25 × 50 cm)

Weft amounts:
☐ 3¹/₄ oz. (92 g) (light)
▨ 1   oz. (28 g) (medium)
■ <u>4</u>   oz. (113 g) (dark)
   8¹/₄ oz. (233 g) total

Warp amount: 50 yards (45.75 m)

Warping particulars:
   Dowel 1 = 41 marks
   Dowel 2 = 40 marks
Warping frame nails:
   18¹/₂" (47 cm) apart

WARP COUNT FOR
DESIGN
3-2-2-2-2-2-2-10 reverse*
3-2-6-2-6-2-6-2-6-2-3
3-14-2-2-2-14-3
15-2-2-2-2-2-15
7-6-2-2-2-2-2-2-2-6-7
7-2-2-2-2-2-2-2-2-2-2-2-2-2-27
7-2-6-2-2-2-2-2-6-2-7
7-2-6-2-6-2-6-2-7
7-26-7
19-2-19
11-6-2-2-2-2-6-11
11-2-2-2-2-2-2-2-2-2-2-11

11-2-6-2-6-2-11
11-18-11

(Four squares = 1" [2.5 cm])

* = reverse sequence
without repeating last number

1 5 10 15 20 25 30 35 40

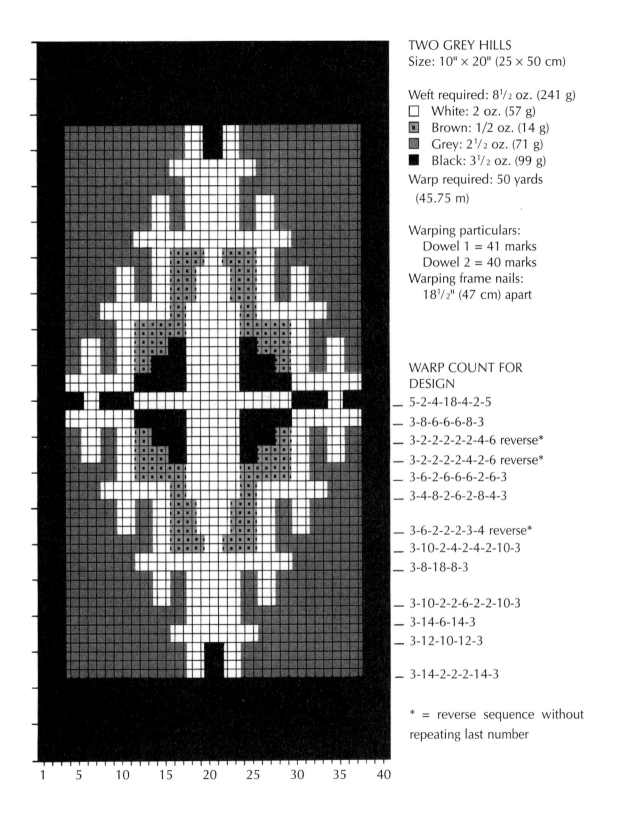

TWO GREY HILLS
Size: 10" × 20" (25 × 50 cm)

Weft required: 8¹/₂ oz. (241 g)
☐ White: 2 oz. (57 g)
▦ Brown: 1/2 oz. (14 g)
▨ Grey: 2¹/₂ oz. (71 g)
■ Black: 3¹/₂ oz. (99 g)
Warp required: 50 yards
  (45.75 m)

Warping particulars:
  Dowel 1 = 41 marks
  Dowel 2 = 40 marks
Warping frame nails:
  18¹/₂" (47 cm) apart

WARP COUNT FOR
DESIGN
— 5-2-4-18-4-2-5
— 3-8-6-6-6-8-3
— 3-2-2-2-2-2-4-6 reverse*
— 3-2-2-2-2-4-2-6 reverse*
— 3-6-2-6-6-6-2-6-3
— 3-4-8-2-6-2-8-4-3

— 3-6-2-2-2-3-4 reverse*
— 3-10-2-4-2-4-2-10-3
— 3-8-18-8-3

— 3-10-2-2-6-2-2-10-3
— 3-14-6-14-3
— 3-12-10-12-3

— 3-14-2-2-2-14-3

* = reverse sequence without
repeating last number

For example, TW 33L means the turning warp is the 33rd warp in from the left edge of the weaving.

2. Marking the turning warp: You may find it useful to mark the turning warp. Loosely tie a piece of string to the turning warp you are using, about 8 inches (20 cm) up from the weaving line. This way, you can easily locate the turning warp and move the marker as the design progresses.

3. Which yarn to start with: When the row is traveling left, start with the yarn on the left. When the row is traveling right, start with the yarn on the right. This means that the yarn you use last when weaving one row will be the one you use first when weaving the next row. Working this way helps eliminate accidental hooking.

4. When to circle a turning warp: When the turning warp is in back (behind the batten), ignore it. When the turning warp is in front, include it.

5. Changing turning warps: When you are using the turned joint to make a shallow diagonal, you will change turning warps continually. In each row your weft will travel one warp farther in the direction in which the design is traveling. Do not worry if wefts sometimes turn around adjacent warps; in the next row, the turning warp will move and the wefts will overlap.

6. Making a smooth diagonal: As shown in the drawing below, to make a smooth diagonal, the decreasing (white) shape should circle the turning warp first.

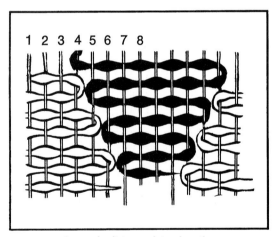

Smooth diagonal in detail.

Basic smooth diagonal shapes requiring the turned joint.

Grace Homer, weaving her design in sections.

They have a ceremony for when someone weaves too much. They grind the white or the yellow corn and just put all the weaving tools in it. A person can tell when to have the ceremony because she gets a headache from weaving.

—Navajo weaver, Tuba City

Combining hooked and turned joints

Navajo weavers often combine hooked and turned joints in the same rug: the hooked joint for verticals, the turned joint for smooth diagonals. Because the joints require different techniques, using them together requires some practice. Working with two joints simultaneously can be an exhilarating experience: success in the face of complexity! However, you should master the techniques separately before trying to put them together.

Diagonal Patterns

There are many variations on weaving the diagonal pattern. Choose your technique based on the kind of edge you want and the inclination of the slope. Remember, both will be influenced by your weft size and the distance between your warps. Also take into consideration the strength of joint you want for your weaving.

The four main diagonal shapes are: the flat diamond (this is the easiest and makes the smoothest edge); the square diamond with stepped edges (as in the sampler, page 102); the square diamond with serrated edges; and the long diamond (which is usually stepped).

Sectioned Weaving

One of the difficulties in weaving a large rug is that the width of your weaving is greater than the length of the batten. The solution is not to get a long, unwieldy batten, for it will tire you. Instead, the Navajo use a technique known as sectioned weaving, sometimes called "lazy line."

In sectioned weaving, a diagonal section is woven. Then an adjoining section is woven to overlap the first section along the diagonal, which raises the weaving to an even line again. The interface between these two sections leaves a subtle diagonal line.

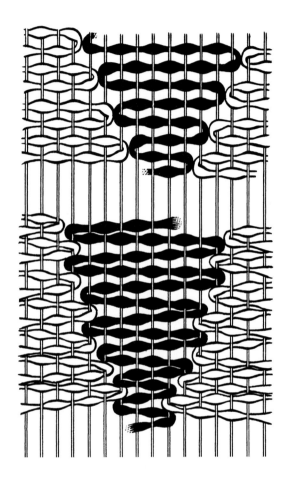

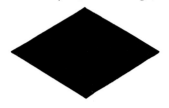

Detail of flat diamond
technique (smooth edge)

Detail of serrated diamond
technique

137

For [excess weaving], have a Blessingway. Yódi bighiin *[soft goods songs] are sung over you: sheep song, spinning song, weaving song, grinding song, beans-of-four-colors song. All things for women.*

—Navajo weaver, The Gap

By weaving the rug in sections, the weaver is able to remain in one position for a period of time—far more efficient than repositioning the weaver and the batten several times for each row.

The sectioned areas are built up diagonally using the turned joint. Each successive row travels one warp more or less than the previous row. The sequence of sectioning is very important. The first section must decrease as it rises to create an open adjacent area. As the adjoining section is woven, it increases to fill the open area and overlap the first section, to form an even weaving line.

Sometimes weavers organize their sections around the pattern, placing the overlaps in the solid background areas. In solid areas the diagonals are not altogether imperceptible in the finished product. If the yarn color varies within a skein, the separately woven adjoining sections emphasize whatever color streaking is present.

To avoid these irregularities, you can coordinate the design and the technique, using sectioned weaving only at the edge of a diagonal pattern where a color change is planned. You can also use this line aesthetically as an intentional color juncture, especially if you are weaving with streaky yarn. This way, you can create subtle nuances within a large unpatterned area.

Finished rug, a variation of Two Grey Hills.

9 The Weaver's Pathway

Some people just weave and weave and weave all the time. And sometimes they think they might just weave their life away. So they put that line in so they can escape. Or they think they might weave themselves into the rug. And they put the line in so they can get out.

—Navajo weaver, Tuba City

Some non-Navajos think it a mistake in the weaving. It occurs in bordered rugs. The Navajo weaver makes a small, contrasting line from background through border to selvage. The line penetrates the border and provides a path through to the outside. The English translation for this line is "The Weaver's Pathway."

The need for a Pathway comes from the box-canyon fear of being enclosed on all sides with no way for escape. The weaver fears that, in channeling all her energies and mental resources into a rug with an enclosing border, she may encircle and thereby entrap her spirit, mind, energies, and design. Her future weaving work is in jeopardy. She must be able to use this design again successfully. Also at risk are her weaving muscles and vision. By vision is meant the ability to see and also the ability to perceive designs—keep them in the mind during weaving. This ability is sometimes equated with "sanity."

In Navajo, two phrases indicate the consequences of weaving a rug with an enclosing border. They are *akii je tło,* "too much weaving," a concept involving sickness of body. And *adaage de tło,* "close yourself in," which can be considered a sickness of mind or spirit.

The Pathway is phasing out because of disuse. In the 1930s it was recorded that roughly seven out of eight rugs contained the line. In 1970 I found one Pathway in every eleven bordered rugs. Today some weavers put it in; most don't.

"I do it all the time."

"Mother did it. I don't put it in, though. I just weave."

"That's old fashioned, and I don't believe in it."

"You don't have to put it in each time—just whenever you remember."

Baskets with Pathways woven in.

You put it in to leave your weaving incomplete, so you never finish. [That way] you can have more weaving experiences and you are open to different designs.

—Navajo weaver, The Gap

One Weaver's Philosophy

Helen Nesbah Tsinnie is a traditional weaver, with a special understanding of how weaving fits into the larger context of life. She describes her method of making a Pathway:

You put the gate [path] in at the top just before you're finished. You use the same color as your background is and you put it through to the outside, then back, then through to the outside, and then back in again. That way it makes four rows.

The Navajos always do things in fours: It's like the four directions: East, South, West, and North. It's like the four sacred mountains that protect us. It's like the four kinds of colors: white, blue or grey, yellow or brown, and black. It's like the four kinds of precious jewels: white shell, turquoise, abalone or coral, and jet. It's like the four horned sheep. It's like the four colors of sheep's wool: white, grey, brown, and black.

So when you make a gateway, just make it with four rows.

Some people do it in different ways. Sometimes a woman makes it one line the first time, two rows the second, three rows the third, and four rows the fourth. Then the next rug she doesn't have to put in any. Like me, now, I just finished the whole group of four with my last rug; this rug won't have any; the next one will have just one row again.

Helen Tsinnie suggests that weaving a Pathway is like asking for the reuse of design. Much energy has gone into the weaving of the blanket. If it's trapped within the border, it can't get out for reuse.

When I put in the line, it's a time to think forward. I just say to myself: "Thank you for letting me use this design and I'd like to use it again sometime." Or other times I say, "Here's to the next rug, may it be even better."

Weaving the Pathway

Pathways are most often woven into rugs in which the inside design is enclosed on all sides by a border. At one point in this border, the weaver inserts a thin, visually broken line of a contrasting color (that of the inside background). This line creates an opening through the border, a Path to the outside of the rug.

There are many ways a Navajo weaver can make this Path. Generally she uses the method her mother and grandmother used. She may be aware that other weavers do it differently, but knows her way to be a good one. Of other weaver's ways, she says:

"Maybe she never learned the right way."

"Maybe she doesn't care about doing it right and so she just does it any old way."

"Maybe she has a different story and that's why she does it that way."

Weaving in the Path strand

The most common way of weaving a Pathway is for a weaver to extend a piece of yarn from the background of the rug through the contrasting border to the selvage. She does this just before she closes the border. She breaks off a background yarn—the Path strand—runs it out to the selvage, and tucks it between the edging cords. The Path strand makes a visual and physical opening through the border (see below).

The Path strand lies in the same shed as a

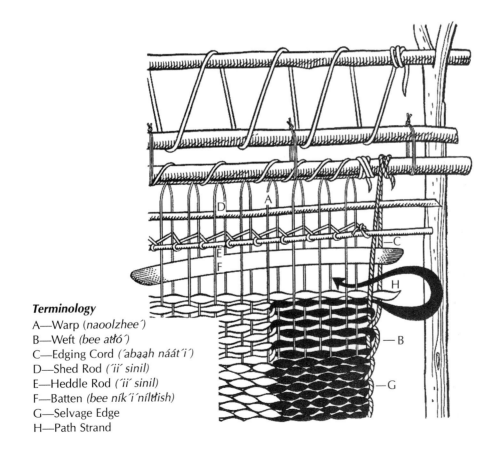

Terminology
A—Warp *(naoolzheeʼ)*
B—Weft *(bee atłóʼ)*
C—Edging Cord *(ʼabąąh nááťiʼ)*
D—Shed Rod *(ʼiiʼ sinil)*
E—Heddle Rod *(ʼiiʼ sinil)*
F—Batten *(bee níkʼiʼníłtłish)*
G—Selvage Edge
H—Path Strand

Without the ch'é'étiin *[pathway] there can be no progress and no improvement.*

—Navajo weaver, Shonto

border weft traveling in the same direction. The border weft returns into the rug; the Path strand does not. Shonto weaver Diane Calamity says:

Take one yarn and let it go through to the outside. Make it smaller than the rest. Put the other yarns in too, then lay this small one on top and let it go out. The other ones can turn around and go back in, not this one.

When the Pathway is two to four rows wide or the entire width of the rug, weavers do not place the Path strand in the shed along with the regular weft. The Path strand goes through alone. Tiana Bighorse says:

First stop all your yarns. Then just break it [the Path strand] off so it's as wide as the rug. Then put your batten in and put in the Path. Just leave the ends there, don't weave them back in. Then take out the batten and put it in the next place [shed]. Put the other yarns back in just like before.

Weave to the South

Navajo weavers traditionally weave the Pathway to the right; to do otherwise is to become involved with the North. Tiana Bighorse says:

Always do it to your right as you sit at the loom, never to your left.

Your left is like the North, and some people say bad things come from the North.

This quotation reminds us that in the Navajo way, we mentally face east; so north is left, and south is to our right.

Where to Position the Pathway

Navajo weavers most often place their Pathways in the top right-hand corner of the border. Some, like Tiana Bighorse, say that the amount of pattern in the weaving determines the position of the Path.

If it's a rug and it doesn't have much pattern in it, then you only have to put a little Path out to the right. But if it [the weaving] has lots of patterns, then I always put the Pathway all the way through the rug.

Navajo weavers generally weave the Pathway in the stick-shed. This is because

Grace Homer, herding her flock.

It's your own path.

It's for yourself.

It's for peace for your future.

It's for the weaver.

—Tiana Bighorse, Tuba City

pulling the heddles forward crosses warps, and the shed is considered closed. But in the stick-shed, warp threads do not cross, and the shed is considered open.

When the Pathway is short and only one row wide, weavers generally put the Path strand in the stick-shed right on top of the regular border weft.

Hidden Pathways

Traders used to see the Pathway and consider it a "flaw" and would pay weavers less for their "imperfect rugs." So some weavers simply hide their Pathways. Tiana tells how her mother did it:

My mother always told me to put it in so it won't show. If your yarn is big, just spin the yarn for the Pathway real little and put it in, then it won't show. You just break it off so it's as wide as the rug. Use the same color as the background; it won't show except maybe just a little as it passes the border.

Visibility is not necessary. The point is, it's for the weaver, and she knows it's there.

How Often to Weave a Pathway

Some weavers say they always weave a Pathway. Tiana Bighorse says:

You don't have to put it in each time—just whenever you remember.

Helen Tsinnie says:

You only have to do it when you weave a rug with a border, not when there are just stripes. The stripes are already a Path. Also if the design touches the edge, you don't need one.

146

Tiana Bighorse.

They say it lets your brain think forward.

—Navajo weaver, Shonto

Diane Calamity says:

My mother did it. I don't put it in though. I just weave.

A Final Thought

To some people, the Pathway may sound like superstition. Young Navajo weavers protest: "I don't put it in and I don't believe I will go blind or crazy." But for anyone who has woven throughout a lifetime and for whom the activity is a source of satisfaction and subsistence, there is very real anxiety that one could become afflicted with illness of eyes, hands, or back. So the Pathway, like prayer, may represent a symbolic way of reducing an ever-present, underlying threat. As well as supplying positive energy to prepare the weaver for the next rug.

It is unfortunate for the younger weavers who hastily liberate themselves from old-time superstition. They also unknowingly deprive themselves of a psychological boost in the creation and planning of the next rug—a boost welcomed by any weaver, Navajo or not. For the moment of Pathway is a moment of liberation, of peace, of security—and a wish for the future:

May the next weaving be even better.

Notes

The information in this book is based on the author's unpublished writings; the working manuscript for her forthcoming book, *Weavers' Notes;* and three previously published books: *Working with the Wool: How to Weave a Navajo Rug; Designing With the Wool: Advanced Techniques in Navajo Weaving;* and *The Weaver's Pathway: A Clarification of the "Spirit Trail" in Navajo Weaving.*

Noël Bennett and Tiana Bighorse are co-authors of *Working with the Wool: How to Weave a Navajo Rug.* Noël is also the author of many articles and several other books including *Halo of the Sun: Stories Told and Retold.*

Introductions:

Introduction by Tiana Bighorse, excerpted from "Keepers of the Culture," edited by Noël Bennett and Sallie Butler-Maloney, *Inter-Tribal America Magazine,* 1994.

Chapter One:

Introduction, adapted from "Navajo Weaving: From the Inside Out," by Noël Bennett, *Four Winds,* Spring 1980.

"Learning to Card," from *Halo of the Sun.*

Chapter Two:

Introduction, adapted from "Navajo Weaving: From the Inside Out," by Noël Bennett, *Four Winds,* Spring 1980.

Specific mordanting instructions, adapted from "Southwest Navajo Dyes," *Natural Plant Dyeing,* Brooklyn Botanic Garden, Brooklyn, NY, 1973.

"Wild Carrot Story," from *Halo of the Sun.*

Chapter Three:

Introduction, adapted from "Navajo Weaving: From the Inside Out," by Noël Bennett, *Four Winds,* Spring 1980.

Chapter Four:

Introduction, adapted from "Navajo Weaving:

From the Inside Out," by Noël Bennett, *Four Winds,* Spring 1980.

Chapter Five:

"Think Forward," excerpted from "Navajo Weaving: From the Inside Out," by Noël Bennett, *Four Winds,* Spring 1980.

Chapter Six:

Introduction, adapted from "Navajo Weaving: From the Inside Out," by Noël Bennett, *Four Winds,* Spring 1980.

Page 96, from *Halo of the Sun.*

Chapter Seven:

Introduction and "Finishing the Rug," adapted from "Navajo Weaving: From the Inside Out," by Noël Bennett, *Four Winds,* Spring 1980.

Chapter Nine:

Introduction, adapted from *Halo of the Sun.*

The loom is a sacred place among weavers. Here women engage in meaningful work that supports their families. Here is dynamic order—colors and shapes continually shifting within a predetermined whole. Here, especially, is an easy exchange of ideas—the place where craft technique, design ideas, and traditions are passed from one to another.

Between 1968 and 1976, twenty-one Navajo weavers sat with me on various occasions at my loom. Or I sat with them at theirs. What they told me in these moments comprise the manuscript for my forthcoming book, *Weavers' Notes,* a collection of legends, taboos, and quotations.

It is important to me that in being with Navajo weavers, ideas are gifted or traded—never purchased. Life blood is not a commodity.

—N.B.

Sources of Information and Supplies

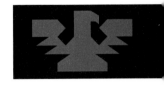

Ashtl'o Weaving Guild
931 Dorel Drive
San Jose, CA 95132
Tel: (408) 259-5594
Contact: Carol Lane
*National organization for people
who weave in the traditional
Navajo way. Quarterly newslet-
ter lists weaving work sessions
and supply sources.*

Cerro Mojino Woolworks
P.O. Box 94
Ojo Caliente, NM 87549
Tel: (505) 986-2952
E-mail: staylor@taos.nmex.com
Contact: Connie Taylor
*Navajo-Churro fleece. Mill-spun
weft in six natural colors from
Navajo-Churro fleece. Custom
dyeing with aniline dyes. Color
matching. Fleece and yarn sam-
ples available.*

Custom Handweavers
2239 Old Middlefield Way, Suite H
Mountain View, CA 94043
Tel: (415) 325-0626
Contact: Hannelore H. Cole
*Classes in Navajo weaving, spin-
ning, and dyeing. Navajo-
Churro fleece and others. Mill-
spun warp. Hardwood looms.
Hardwood forks. Carders.
Spindles. Sacking needles. Books.*

Damascus Pioneer Craft School
14711 S.E. Anderson Road
Clackamas, OR 97015

Tel: (503) 658-2704
*Classes taught by Audrey Moore, all
levels. Navajo-Churro fleece and
others. Cushing Navajo aniline
dyes. Davidson's Navajo mill-spun
warp. Single-ply weft, mill-spun by
Harrisville (Designer) and Brown
Sheep Company. Cedar looms, up
to 72 inches (183 cm) or custom
sizes. Oak and other hardwood
forks with pointed handles.
Curved oak or other hardwood
battens. Books. Semi-annual class
schedule available.*

Davidson Corporation
Eaton Rapids, MI 48827
Tel: (800) 222-2711
Four-ply mill-spun Navajo warp.

Duncan Fiber Enterprises
21740 S.E. Edward Drive
Clackamas, OR 97015
Tel: (503) 658-4066
Contact: Dick and Joane Duncan
*Navajo looms of kiln-dried western
red cedar, standard size 72 inch-
es (183 cm) or custom sizes.*

Harrisville Designs
P.O. Box 806
Harrisville, NH 03450
Tel: (800) 338-9415
*Single-ply mill-spun weft, commer-
cially dyed.*

Hillcreek Fiber Studio
7001 Hillcreek Road
Columbia, MO 65203

Tel: (573) 874-2233
To order: (800) 874-9328
Contact: Carol Leigh Brack-Kaiser
*Beginning Navajo Weaving Classes.
Warp and weft. Medium and
large looms. Forks with pointed
handles, including finishing
forks. Curved oak battens. Books.
Cassette: "Patterns of Power,"
Noël Bennett's 1982 Convergence
keynote. Catalog available.*

Howell's Weaving Emporium
4832 Salmon Drive
Paradise, CA 95969
Tel: (916) 877-4539
Looms. Forks.

Idyllwild Arts
P.O. Box 38
52500 Temecula Road
Idyllwild, CA 92549
Tel: (909) 659-2171 x371
Fax: (909) 659-5463
Contact: Heather S. Companiott,
Coordinator, Native Arts Program
*Navajo weaving classes by Navajo
weavers Rainbow Stevens,
Juanita Stevens, and Alita Begay.*

La Casa Cien
P.O. Box 580
Las Luz, NM 88337
Tel: (505) 437-5169
Contact: F.M. Herrera
*Navajo weaving classes, all levels.
Davidson's Navajo mill-spun
warp. Pine pole or lumber
looms, up to 8 feet (2.5 m). Oak*

151

forks with pointed handles. Handmade spindles. Sacking needles, 6 inches (15 cm). Handmade needles (substitutes for umbrella ribs), up to 36 inches (91 cm) long. Cotton rope and twine.

La Lana Wools

136 Paseo Norte
Taos, NM 87571
Tel: (505) 758-9631
Contact: Luisa Gelenter
Navajo weaving and plant dyeing classes taught by Navajo weaver Kalley Musial. Navajo-Churro fleece and others. Navajo plant dyes, including Hopi Tea and Snakeweed. Single-ply hand-spun weft, plant-dyed only. Single-ply mill-spun warp. Schacht Navajo spindles. Ungrooved umbrella ribs.

Sarah and Leo Natani

P.O. Box 2465
Shiprock, NM 87420
Navajo weaving classes, all levels, taught on the Navajo Reservation at Sarah's home. Navajo-Churro fleece. Navajo plant dyes, including Navajo Tea and Wild Carrot. Pine looms. Handmade hardwood forks and curved battens of Scrub and Fendler's Oak.

Navajo Community College

Office of Continuing Education
P.O. Box 731
Tuba City, AZ 86045
Tel: (520) 283-6321
Navajo weaving classes taught by Navajo weavers.

Puddleduck Farm

25782 Timber Road
Brownsville, OR 97327
Tel: (541) 466-3203
E-mail: Puddleduck@proaxis.com

Contact: Alan and Ingrid Painter
Navajo Churro fleece and others. Mill-spun warp. Mill-spun weft, fine and medium weights, in black, grey, and brown.

Rio Grande Weavers Supply

216-B Pueblo Norte
Taos, NM 87571
Tel: (505) 758-0433
Fax: (505) 758-5839
Contact: Rachel Brown
One-ply to four-ply mill-spun warp. Single-ply mill-spun weft in all weights, 20 commercially dyed and more than 70 hand-dyed colors. Some yarns of New Mexico Navajo-Churro; most of New Zealand wool. Alderwood Navajo looms in three sizes up to 89 inches (2.25 m). Maple forks with pointed handles. Curved maple or Alderwood battens. Schacht spindles. Sacking needles, 5 sizes up to 8 inches (20 cm). Books. Color catalog available.

R.B. Burnham and Co.

Sanders, AZ 86512
Tel: (602) 688-2777
Single-ply mill-spun weft, commercially dyed in about 20 colors.

Salt Lake Weaver's Store

1227 East 3300 South
Salt Lake City, UT 84106
Tel: (801) 486-1610
To order: (800) 363-5585
Contact: Annie Taylor
Navajo weaving classes taught by Riki Darling. Burnham single-ply weft. Looms. Forks, some with pointed handles.

Tierra Wools

P.O. Box 295
Los Ojos, NM 87551
Tel: (505) 588-7044
Raw and carded Churro fleece.

Single-ply yarns, handspun and mill-spun, hand-dyed with natural dyes.

Taos Institute of Arts

P.O. Box 5280 NDCBU
Taos, NM 87571
Tel: (505) 758-2793
Contact: Judith Krull, Associate Director
Navajo weaving classes, all levels, taught by Navajo weavers Pearl Sunrise, Sarah Natani, and the Bizahaloni family.

Village Wools

3801 C. San Mateo N.E.
Albuquerque, NM 87110
Tel: (505) 883-2919
Contact: Cathlena Burr, Susan Lupton
Navajo weaving classes taught by Navajo weaver Pearl Sunrise. Navajo Churro fleece and others. Some native plant dyes. Handmade pine-log looms and tools made by Pearl Sunrise's family, including oak and cedar curved battens, forks with pointed handles, and spindles. Umbrella ribs.

Wild West Weaver

54 Danbury Road, Suite 248
Ridgefield, CT 06877
Tel: (203) 431-5717
Web site: http://members.aol.com/wwweaver1
Contact: Leslie Smith Jackson
Navajo-Churro fleece. Navajo warp. Fine and medium single-ply weft, some mill-spun of Navajo sheep. Navajo-made cedar and oak forks. Navajo-made battens, 1 inch (2.5 cm) wide, in three lengths. Books and music.

Glossary of Terms

Batten: A smooth, flat, wooden tool used to keep the shed open while a weft is inserted.

Bowline knot (or weaver's knot): A non-slipping knot useful for beginning and ending the warping process and for repairing a broken warp. (See also page 69.)

Bubbling: See Scalloping.

Edging cord: Two-ply handspun yarn used as binding at the top and bottom of the weaving. (See also selvage cord.)

Heddle rod: A tool used to reverse the warp position of the stick-shed. The rod is placed horizontally in front of the warps; string is looped from the rod to the warps behind the upper shed rod. When the heddle rod is pulled, the back warps come forward to create the "pull-shed."

Hooked joint (or interlocking weft, weft lock, or weft join): The method of joining two weft colors by hooking them. This joint occurs between warps and does not reduce the strength of the final woven product. (See also page 104.)

Interlocking warp: See Turned joint.

Interlocking weft: See Hooked joint.

Laying in (as of yarn): A method of introducing a new weft yarn by trailing a tapered end through the shed until it is just inside the new design area.

Overlapping joint: The method of piecing two weft yarns by overlapping their tapered ends in the shed.

Pull-shed: The opening between the front and back warps created by separating the two shed rods and pulling on the heddle rod. In this manner, back warps are brought into a forward position. A batten is inserted to increase the warp separation before the weft is inserted.

Rolag: Combed fleece that has been removed from the carders in the form of a loose roll.

Scalloping (or bubbling): The process of laying weft loosely in the shed so as to control weft tension.

Selvage cord: Two-ply handspun yarn used as binding on the edges of the weaving in the selvage positions.

Shed: The opening between the front and back warps into which a weft is inserted. The shed is created by manipulating the rods and is held open by the batten turned on edge.

Shed rod (or upper shed rod): The stick located behind alternate warps to hold every other warp forward. The shed rod creates the opening into which a batten is inserted to form the "stick-shed."

Square knot: The basic knot usually used in Navajo weaving, but which is more likely to slip than the recommended bowline knot.

Stick-shed: The opening between the front and back warps created by positioning the shed and heddle rods together. A batten, inserted below the rods, holds the warps apart so that the weft can be inserted.

Stick-shuttle: A dry straight twig with broken ends on which the weft is wrapped, and by means of which the weft is carried through the shed from one side of the weaving to the other in areas of solid stripe.

Tapestry weave: The most common Navajo weave structure. Wefts travel over and under alternate warps and are beaten firmly so as to completely cover the warps.

Turned joint (or interlocking warp, warp lock, or warp join): The method of joining two weft colors by turning the wefts around a common warp. (See also page 104.)

Two-ply yarn: Two single strands of yarn that are twisted together in a direction opposite to that of the original yarn-spin. Two-ply yarns serve as edging and selvage cords.

Upper shed rod: See Shed rod.

Warp: The fine, tightly spun yarn initially tied onto the loom in ten-sion before the weaving begins. Also refers to the individual warp yarns.

Warp join: See Turned joint.

Warp lock: See Turned joint.

Warp pair: See Warp turn.

Warp turn (or warp pair): During the warping process, when a warp yarn is carried over a dowel and returned back toward the weaver, the two sections of yarn form a warp turn, or warp pair. These two warps are treated as a unit during the edging and binding processes and in the first and final four rows of the weaving.

Weaver's knot: See Bowline knot.

Weaving line: The horizontal line in which the weft travels across the warp.

Weft: The softly spun yarn that is woven over and under the warp from one side of the weaving to the other.

Weft join: See Hooked joint.

Weft lock: See Hooked joint.

Suggested Readings

If you're tired of weaving but not of dreaming. . .

If you're looking for inspiration on your next weaving. . .

If you've run out of yarn and find it difficult to await replacement,

then perhaps this reading guide can help you through.

Adrosko, Rita J. *Natural Dyes and Home Dyeing*. New York: Dover, 1971.

Amsden, Charles Avery. *Navajo Weaving; Its Technic and Its History*. The Fine Arts Press, 1934. Reprint. Chicago: Rio Grande Press, 1964.

Bennett, Noël. *Designing with the Wool: Advanced Techniques in Navajo Weaving*. Flagstaff, AZ: Northland Press, 1979.

———. "Navajo Weaving: From the Inside Out," *Four Winds: The International Forum for Native American Art, Literature, and History*, Spring 1980.

———. *Genuine Navajo Rug: How to Tell*. Museum of Navajo Ceremonial Art and the Navajo Tribe, 1973. Reprint. Palmer Lake, CO: Filter Press, in cooperation with the IACA, 1979.

———. *Halo of the Sun: Stories Told and Retold*. Flagstaff, AZ: Northland Press, 1987.

———. "Power and Understatement," *Oriental Rug Review* Vol. 8, No. 6, Aug/Sept 1988.

———. *The Weaver's Pathway: A Clarification of the "Spirit Trail" in Navajo Weaving*. Flagstaff, AZ: Northland Press, 1974.

Bennett, Noël, and Tiana Bighorse. *Working with the Wool: How to Weave a Navajo Rug*. Flagstaff: Northland Press, 1971.

———. "Painted Desert / Woven Desert," *Oriental Rug Review* Vol. 8, No. 6, Aug/Sept 1988. Article on pictorial tapestry woven by Tiana Bighorse.

Berlant, Anthony, and Mary Hunt Kahlenberg. *Walk in Beauty: The Navajo and Their Blankets*. Boston: New York Graphic Society, 1977.

Bighorse, Tiana. "Weaving the Navajo Way." Edited by Noël Bennett. *Interweave*. Winter 1978-79.

———. *Bighorse the Warrior*. Edited by Noël Bennett. Tucson: University of Arizona, 1990.

———. "Keepers of the Culture." Edited by Noël Bennett and Sallie Butler-Maloney. *Inter-Tribal America Magazine*. Gallup, NM: Inter-Tribal Indian Ceremonial Association, 1994.

Blomberg, Nancy J. *Navajo Textiles: The William Randolph Hearst Collection*. Tucson: University of Arizona Press, 1988.

Blood, Charles L., and Martin Link. *Goat in the Rug*. New York: Parents' Magazine Press, 1976.

Bonar, Eulalie H., ed. *Woven By the Grandmothers: Nineteenth Century Navajo Textiles from the National Museum of the American Indian*. Washington, DC: Smithsonian Institution Press, 1996.

Brako, Jeanne, and Robert Morgan. "The Care of Navajo Textiles in the Home." *Terra* 26:5 (1988): 21–24.

Brandon, Marilyn. *From Wool to Navajo Rug*. Scotts Valley, CA: M.J., 1990.

Brody, J.J. *Between Traditions: Navajo Weaving Toward the End of the Nineteenth Century*. Iowa City: University of Iowa Museum of Art, 1976.

Brown, Rachel. *The Weaving, Spinning and Dyeing Book*. 2nd edition. New York: Knopf, 1983. Contains chapter entitled "Weaving on a Navajo Loom."

Bryan, Nonabah, and Stella Young. *Navajo Native Dyes: Their Preparation and Use*. Lawrence, KS: Haskell Institute, United States Department of the Interior, 1940.

Cerny, Charlene. *Navajo Pictorial Weaving*. Santa Fe: Museum of New Mexico Press, 1974.

Colton, Mary-Russell Ferrell. *Hopi Dyes*. Flagstaff, AZ: The Museum of Northern Arizona, 1965.

Dedera, Don. *Navajo Rugs: How to Find, Evaluate, Care for Them*. Flagstaff, AZ: Northland Press, 1975.

Dockstader, Frederick J. *Weaving Arts of the North American Indian*. New York: Thomas Y. Crowell, 1978.

———. *The Song of the Loom: New Traditions in Navajo Weaving*. New York: Hudson Hills Press, 1987.

El Palacio. *Navajo Weaving Handbook*. Santa Fe: Museum of New Mexico Press, 1974.

Ericksen, Jon T., and N. Thomas Cain. *Navajo Textiles: From the Read Mullen Collection*. Phoenix, AZ: The Heard Museum, 1976.

Getzweiler, Steve. *Ray Manley's The Fine Art of Navajo Weaving*. Tucson, AZ: Ray Manley Publishing, 1984.

Harvey, Byron. *The Fred Harvey Fine Arts Collection*. Phoenix, AZ: The Heard Museum, 1976.

Hedlund, Ann Lane. *Beyond The Loom: Keys to Understanding Early Southwestern Weaving*. Introduction and observations by Joe Ben Wheat. Boulder: Johnson Books, 1990.

———. *Reflections of the Weaver's World: The Gloria F. Ross Collection of Contemporary Navajo Weaving*. Denver: Denver Art Museum, 1992.

———. *Contemporary Navajo Weaving: Thoughts That Count*. Flagstaff, AZ: Museum of Northern Arizona Press, 1994.

Hedlund, Ann Lane, and Louise I. Stiver. "Wedge Weave Textiles of the Navajo." *American Indian Art Magazine* 16(3) (1991): 54–65, 82.

Hollister, U.S. *The Navajo and His Blanket*. 1903. Reprint. Chicago: Rio Grande Press, 1937.

James, George Wharton. *Indian Blankets and Their Makers*. A.C. McClurg and Co., 1914. Reprint. Chicago: Rio Grande Press, 1937.

James, H.L. *Rugs and Posts: The Story of Navajo Rugs and Their Homes*. Globe, AZ: Southwest Parks and Monuments Association, 1976.

Jongeward, David. *Weaver of Worlds: From Navajo Apprenticeship to Sacred Geometry and Dreams—A Woman's Journey in Tapestry*. Rochester, VT: Destiny Books, 1990.

Kaufman, Alice, and Christopher Selser. *Navajo Weaving Tradition: 1650 to Present*. New York, NY: NAL/Dutton, 1985.

Kent, Kate Peck. *Navajo Weaving: Three Centuries of Change*. Santa Fe, NM: School of American Research Press, 1985.

McQuiston, Don, and Debra McQuiston. *Woven Spirit of the Southwest*. San Francisco, CA: Chronicle Books, 1995.

Reichard, Gladys A. *Weaving A Navajo Blanket*. J.J. Augustin, 1936. Reprint. New York: Dover Publications, Inc., 1974. Original edition entitled *Navajo Shepherd and Weaver*.

Rodee, Marian. *Old Navajo Rugs*. Albuquerque: University of New Mexico Press, 1981.

———. *Weaving of the Southwest*. Albuquerque: University of New Mexico Press, 1977.

Roessel, Monty. *Songs From the Loom: A Navajo Girl Learns to Weave*. Minneapolis, MN: Lerner Publications, 1995.

Schiffer, Nancy N. *Navajo Weaving Today*. West Chester, PA: Schiffer Publishing, 1991.

———. *Pictorial Weavings of the Navajo*. West Chester, PA: Schiffer Publishing, 1991.

Wheat, Joe Ben. *Navajo Blankets From the Collection of Anthony Berlant*. Tucson, AZ: The University of Arizona Museum of Art, 1974.

———. "The Navajo Chief Blanket." *American Indian Art*. Summer 1976.

Wheat, Joe Ben, and H. P. Mera. *The Alfred I. Barton Collection of Southwestern Textiles*. Miami, FL: The Lowe Art Museum, University of Miami, 1978.

———. *The Gift of Spiderwoman: Southwestern Textiles, The Navajo Tradition*. Philadelphia, PA: The University Museum, University of Pennsylvania, 1984.

Willink, Roseann Sandoval, and Paul G. Zolbrod. *Weaving a World: Textiles and the Navajo Way of Seeing*. Santa Fe, NM: Museum of New Mexico Press, 1996.

Index

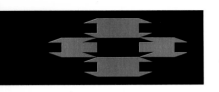# About the Authors

Noël Kirkish Bennett was born in California in 1939. She graduated cum laude from Stanford University (B.A. 1961, Art with Honors in Humanities; M.A. 1962, Fine Arts and Education) and taught at the College of Notre Dame and University of New Mexico.

Noël began her life on the Navajo reservation when her physician-husband joined the Public Health Service in 1968. In Tuba City, Arizona, she studied weaving under the tutelage of twenty-one Navajo weavers and learned the whole spectrum of the craft: shearing the sheep, plant-dyeing the wool, carding, spinning, and weaving. After two years in Tuba City, she moved to Shonto, about an hour away, where her husband set up a full-time medical station for Navajos living in this remote area. In Shonto, her understanding of weaving deepened, as she was able to compare notes with weavers there.

Today Noël lives, writes, and paints in the Jemez Mountains of New Mexico in an experimental straw-bale house that she built in collaboration with her partner Jim Wakeman.

Tiana Bighorse was born in 1917 north of Tuba City, Arizona, to the Deer Spring Clan. At the age of seven, she started school at Tuba City Boarding School and she started to weave. Whereas her school career lasted through the ninth grade (a remarkable achievement for a Navajo of her generation), her weaving career has lasted almost three-quarters of a century.

Tiana's mother, Bertha Whitehair Bighorse, taught her the weaving skill, just as she had been taught by her mother before her. Tiana's mother wove large rugs. She was very mindful of their quality and passed on this pride to her daughter.

Although Tiana's married name is Butler, she chooses to use the name Bighorse in honor of her father, Gus Bighorse, "a brave and courageous man, who defended the Navajo land against Spaniards, Mexicans, and the Cavalry." Her father, named for the size of his horses, lived a strong life until he died at the age of ninety-two. "He always liked his name, Bighorse."

Tiana Bighorse has lived her life on the western side of the reservation in the Tuba City area.